KING

3

WRITTEN AND DRAWN BY
HO CHE ANDERSON

Regardless of its basis as truth or myth, Kennedy's legacy was that of a media created *Camelot*, of a man equal parts visionary, statesman and knight, passionately committed to his vision of America and its dream.

For many Americans...I daresay for all of us, Black and White, that particular dream was shattered on the 22nd of November in 1963.

I remember the entire period with profound clarity, us riveted to our television for three days and nights, watching the spectacle unfold, my sons and I. The limousine driving along the triangle at Dealey Plaza—

—The assassination, the arrest of Lee Harvey Oswald and *his* subsequent "execution" at the hands of Dallas strip club owner, Jack Ruby...a distraught LBJ taking the oath of office on Air Force One—

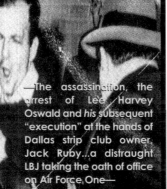

—With Jacqueline Kennedy in *shock*, still dressed in blood-stained clothes, standing beside him. And so, the former Texas senator, former Vice-President Lyndon Baines Johnson, became *President* by default.

My conctact with King at that time was, to put it charitably, minimal. I know from mutual friends that the death of JFK was one of the worst things that could have happened to him politically.

Kennedy's door had always been open to him, and King's influence on JFK was reflected clearly to anybody who knew to look....

I've even heard that had Kennedy lived, King would have reversed his policy and endorsed him for re-election in '64. The bald facts are that in JFK, King had a powerful ally.

I'll grant that Johnson seemed committed to correcting the social ills of civil-rights, that's not in question, but it's also true that he had yet to avail himself in King's eyes.

In St. Augustine, Florida, Klan activity reached an all-time high, to the point where law had effectively ceased to exist for the Blacks of that area. What you have to understand about St. Augustine was that the place was probably the most permanent European community in North America.

Let me tell you something, those days I had no vices to speak of, I didn't smoke, didn't drink, didn't chase no women. All I did was beat and lynch niggers, Saturday nights.

I mean, god*damn*.... Heh, I guess you never smelled a nigger burn.... You should, though, it's an experience, 's easily one'o nature's sweetest smells, I don't mean to offend the ladies—

The SCLC set up demonstrations there in April of '64 which turned into a violent nightmare. A stalemate was eventually met between the segregationists and the demonstrators. The Johnson administration was reluctant to do anything to help at first, *refusing* to send in federal marshals to intervene—

—But eventually, partly as a tribute to the late Kennedy, partly to get the demonstrations over with, on July 2, King and other Black leaders were on hand in the east ballroom of the White House when LBJ signed into law the civil-rights bill that JFK had been trying to get off the ground.

Supposedly this was the farthest reaching civil-rights legislation since the *reconstruction*. It *guaranteed* Blacks the right to vote and access to public accomodations—it also authorized the federal government to sue if necessary to desegregate public facilities and schools.

Afterward, Johnson reasoned the need for direct action protest was over. He actually believed that the civil rights act eliminated the last vestiges of injustice in our *beloved* America. OK...perhaps discrimination was now *technically* illegal....

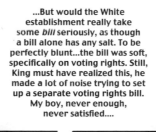

...But would the White establishment really take some *bill* seriously, as though a bill alone has any salt. To be perfectly blunt...the bill was soft, specifically on voting rights. Still, King must have realized this, he made a lot of noise trying to set up a separate voting rights bill. My boy, never enough, never satisfied....

It's no secret Martin King and J. Edgar Hoover *despised* each other. King enraged Hoover when he publicly criticized the FBI—when *Time* named King Man of the Year, Hoover's said to have responded, "They had to dig deep in the garbage for this one." This about a Nobel Laureate. It was the March on Washington that convinced Hoover the Civil Rights Movement wouldn't go away on its own, that he'd have to smash it to preserve his America.

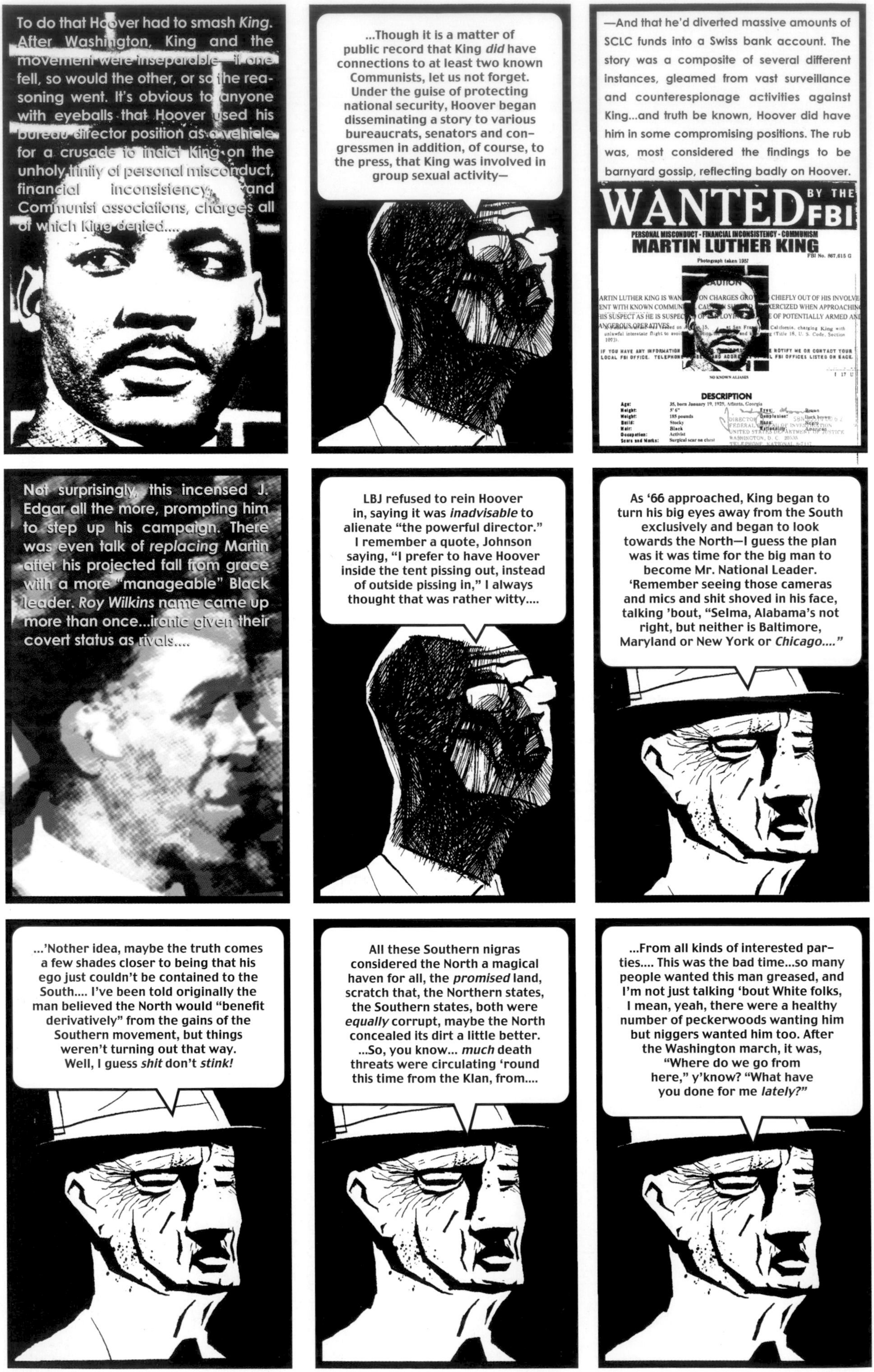
To do that Hoover had to smash *King*. After Washington, King and the movement were inseparable—if one fell, so would the other, or so the reasoning went. It's obvious to anyone with eyeballs that Hoover used his bureau director position as a vehicle for a crusade to indict King on the unholy trinity of personal misconduct, financial inconsistency, and Communist associations, charges all of which King denied....
...Though it is a matter of public record that King *did* have connections to at least two known Communists, let us not forget. Under the guise of protecting national security, Hoover began disseminating a story to various bureaucrats, senators and congressmen in addition, of course, to the press, that King was involved in group sexual activity—
—And that he'd diverted massive amounts of SCLC funds into a Swiss bank account. The story was a composite of several different instances, gleamed from vast surveillance and counterespionage activities against King...and truth be known, Hoover did have him in some compromising positions. The rub was, most considered the findings to be barnyard gossip, reflecting badly on Hoover.
WANTED BY THE FBI
PERSONAL MISCONDUCT - FINANCIAL INCONSISTENCY - COMMUNISM
MARTIN LUTHER KING
FBI No. 867,615 G
Photograph taken 1957
NO KNOWN ALIASES
DESCRIPTION
Age: 35, born January 19, 1929, Atlanta, Georgia
Height: 5' 6"
Weight: 185 pounds
Build: Stocky
Hair: Black
Occupation: Activist
Scars and Marks: Surgical scar on chest
Eyes: Brown
Complexion: Dark brown
Race: Negro
Nationality: American
Not surprisingly, this incensed J. Edgar all the more, prompting him to step up his campaign. There was even talk of *replacing* Martin after his projected fall from grace with a more "manageable" Black leader. *Roy Wilkins* name came up more than once...ironic given their covert status as rivals....
LBJ refused to rein Hoover in, saying it was *inadvisable* to alienate "the powerful director." I remember a quote, Johnson saying, "I prefer to have Hoover inside the tent pissing out, instead of outside pissing in," I always thought that was rather witty....
As '66 approached, King began to turn his big eyes away from the South exclusively and began to look towards the North—I guess the plan was it was time for the big man to become Mr. National Leader. 'Remember seeing those cameras and mics and shit shoved in his face, talking 'bout, "Selma, Alabama's not right, but neither is Baltimore, Maryland or New York or *Chicago....*"
...'Nother idea, maybe the truth comes a few shades closer to being that his ego just couldn't be contained to the South.... I've been told originally the man believed the North would "benefit derivatively" from the gains of the Southern movement, but things weren't turning out that way. Well, I guess *shit* don't *stink!*
All these Southern nigras considered the North a magical haven for all, the *promised* land, scratch that, the Northern states, the Southern states, both were *equally* corrupt, maybe the North concealed its dirt a little better. ...So, you know... *much* death threats were circulating 'round this time from the Klan, from....
...From all kinds of interested parties.... This was the bad time...so many people wanted this man greased, and I'm not just talking 'bout White folks, I mean, yeah, there were a healthy number of peckerwoods wanting him but niggers wanted him too. After the Washington march, it was, "Where do we go from here," y'know? "What have you done for me *lately?*"

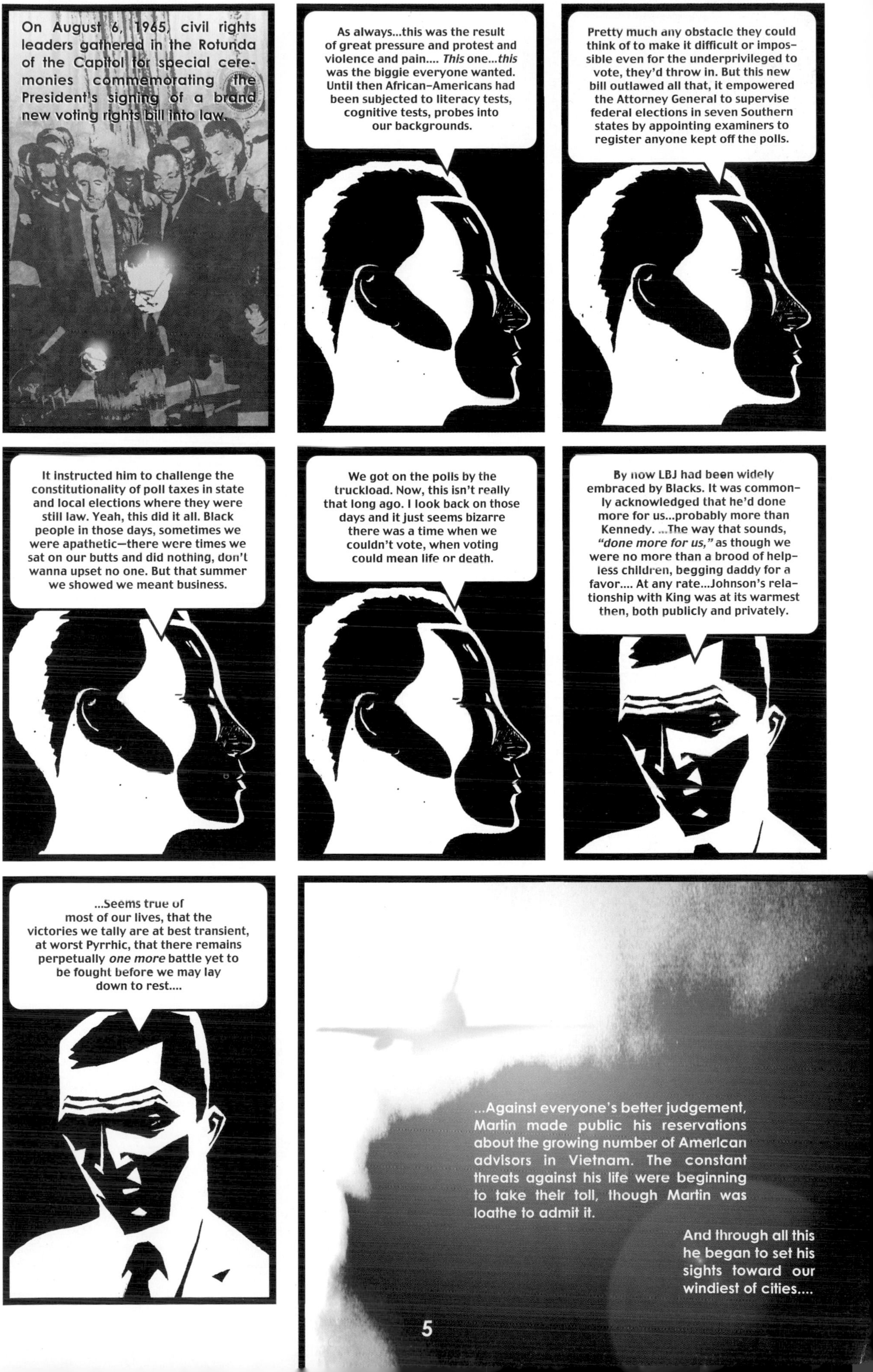
On August 6, 1965, civil rights leaders gathered in the Rotunda of the Capitol for special ceremonies commemorating the President's signing of a brand new voting rights bill into law.
As always...this was the result of great pressure and protest and violence and pain.... *This* one...*this* was the biggie everyone wanted. Until then African-Americans had been subjected to literacy tests, cognitive tests, probes into our backgrounds.
Pretty much any obstacle they could think of to make it difficult or impossible even for the underprivileged to vote, they'd throw in. But this new bill outlawed all that, it empowered the Attorney General to supervise federal elections in seven Southern states by appointing examiners to register anyone kept off the polls.
It instructed him to challenge the constitutionality of poll taxes in state and local elections where they were still law. Yeah, this did it all. Black people in those days, sometimes we were apathetic—there were times we sat on our butts and did nothing, don't wanna upset no one. But that summer we showed we meant business.
We got on the polls by the truckload. Now, this isn't really that long ago. I look back on those days and it just seems bizarre there was a time when we couldn't vote, when voting could mean life or death.
By now LBJ had been widely embraced by Blacks. It was commonly acknowledged that he'd done more for us...probably more than Kennedy. ...The way that sounds, *"done more for us,"* as though we were no more than a brood of helpless children, begging daddy for a favor.... At any rate...Johnson's relationship with King was at its warmest then, both publicly and privately.
...Seems true of most of our lives, that the victories we tally are at best transient, at worst Pyrrhic, that there remains perpetually *one more* battle yet to be fought before we may lay down to rest....
...Against everyone's better judgement, Martin made public his reservations about the growing number of American advisors in Vietnam. The constant threats against his life were beginning to take their toll, though Martin was loathe to admit it.
And through all this he began to set his sights toward our windiest of cities....

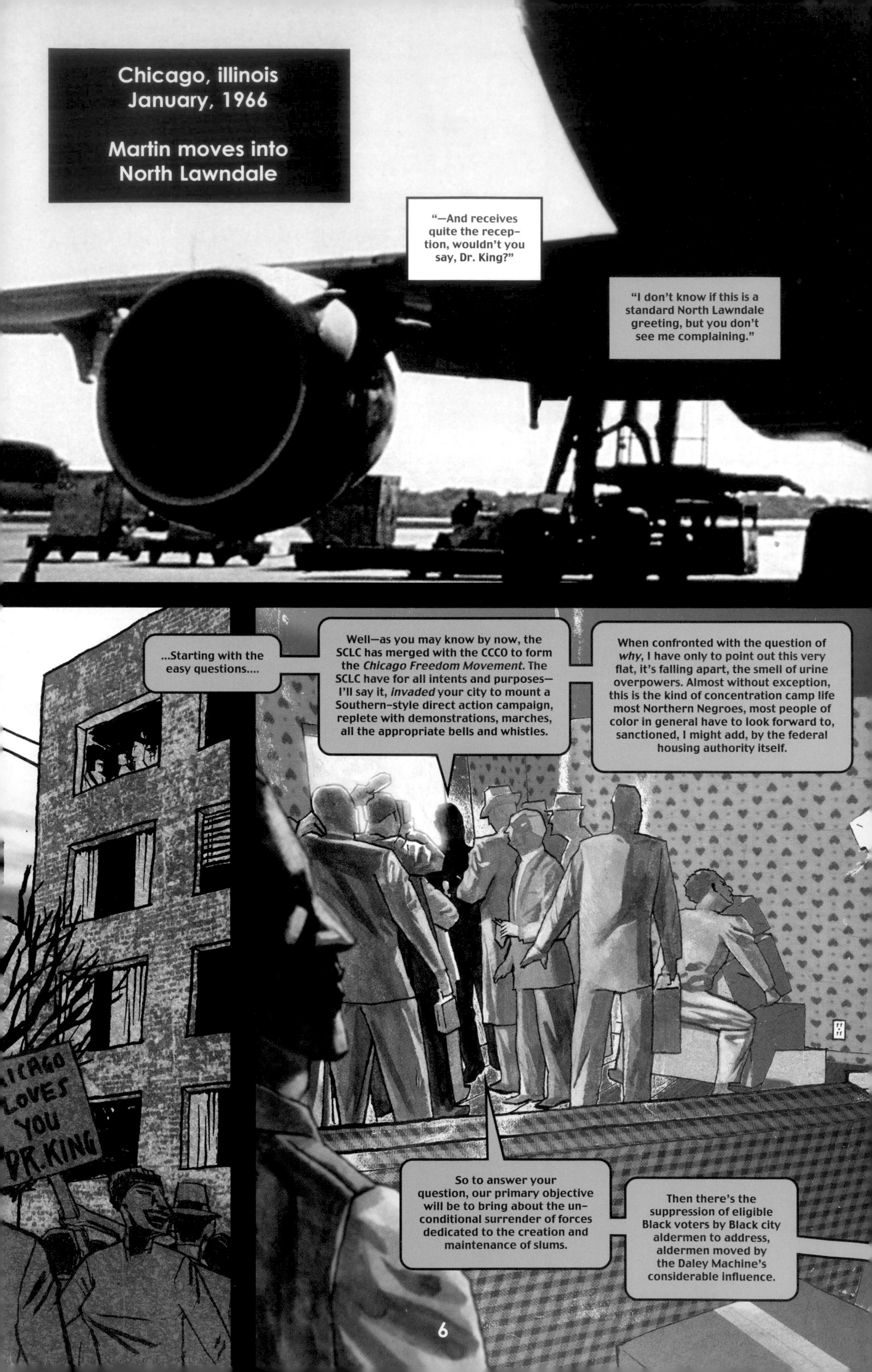

Chicago, illinois
January, 1966
Martin moves into North Lawndale
"—And receives quite the reception, wouldn't you say, Dr. King?"
"I don't know if this is a standard North Lawndale greeting, but you don't see me complaining."
...Starting with the easy questions....
Well—as you may know by now, the SCLC has merged with the CCCO to form the *Chicago Freedom Movement*. The SCLC have for all intents and purposes—I'll say it, *invaded* your city to mount a Southern-style direct action campaign, replete with demonstrations, marches, all the appropriate bells and whistles.
When confronted with the question of *why*, I have only to point out this very flat, it's falling apart, the smell of urine overpowers. Almost without exception, this is the kind of concentration camp life most Northern Negroes, most people of color in general have to look forward to, sanctioned, I might add, by the federal housing authority itself.
ICAGO LOVES YOU DR. KING
So to answer your question, our primary objective will be to bring about the unconditional surrender of forces dedicated to the creation and maintenance of slums.
Then there's the suppression of eligible Black voters by Black city aldermen to address, aldermen moved by the Daley Machine's considerable influence.

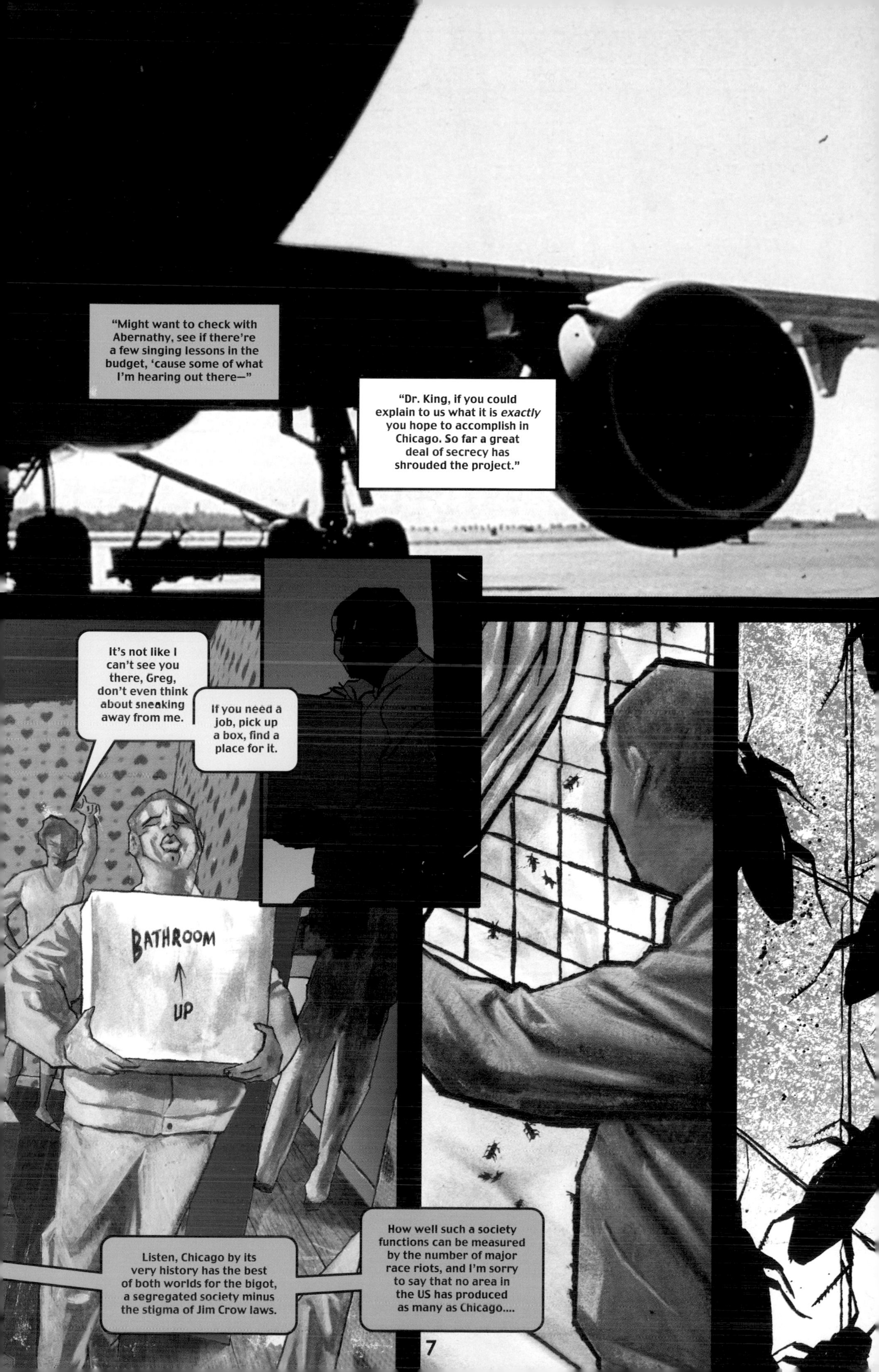

"Might want to check with Abernathy, see if there're a few singing lessons in the budget, 'cause some of what I'm hearing out there—"
"Dr. King, if you could explain to us what it is *exactly* you hope to accomplish in Chicago. So far a great deal of secrecy has shrouded the project."
It's not like I can't see you there, Greg, don't even think about sneaking away from me.
If you need a job, pick up a box, find a place for it.
BATHROOM
UP
Listen, Chicago by its very history has the best of both worlds for the bigot, a segregated society minus the stigma of Jim Crow laws.
How well such a society functions can be measured by the number of major race riots, and I'm sorry to say that no area in the US has produced as many as Chicago....

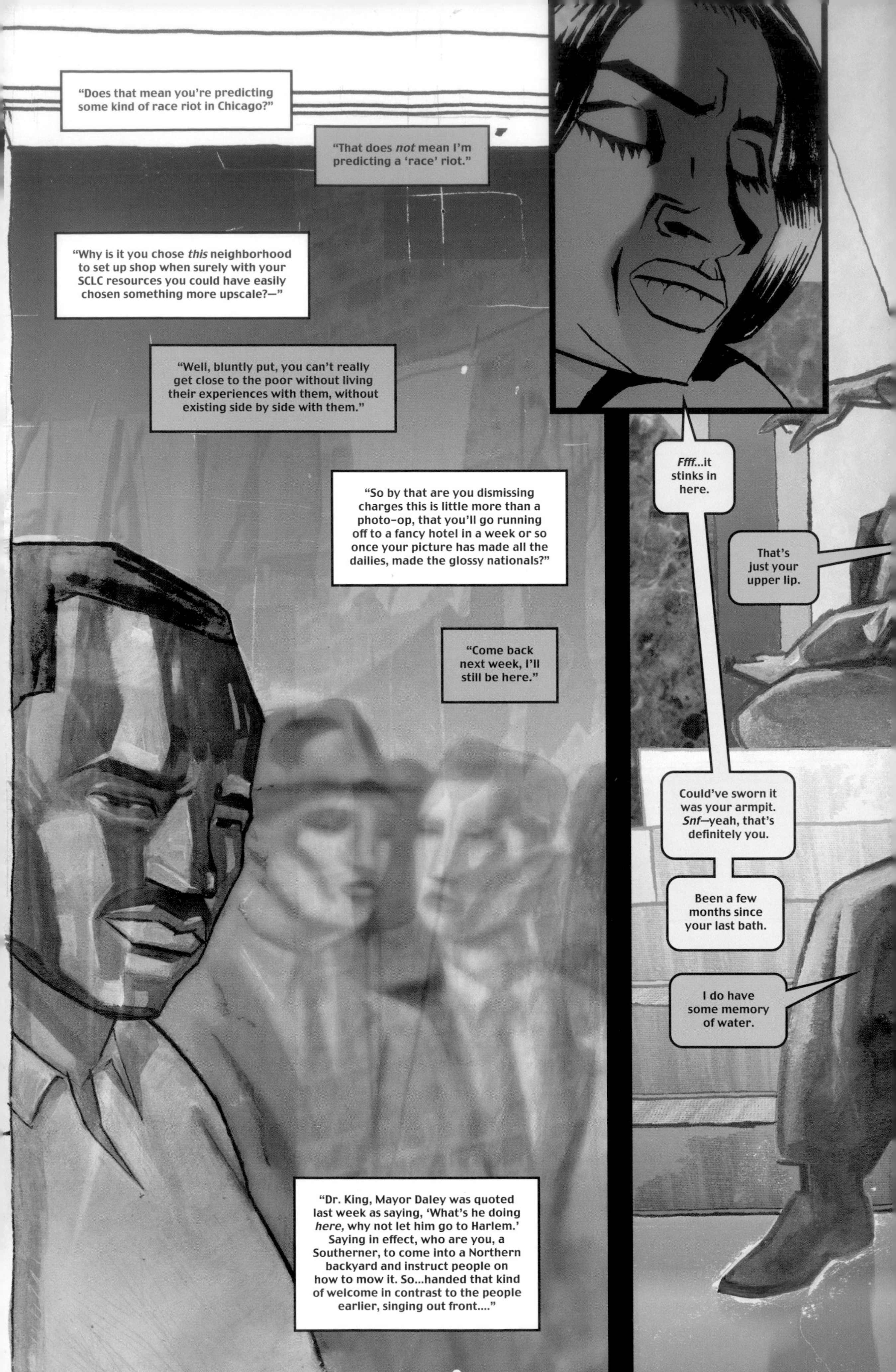
"Does that mean you're predicting some kind of race riot in Chicago?"
"That does *not* mean I'm predicting a 'race' riot."
"Why is it you chose *this* neighborhood to set up shop when surely with your SCLC resources you could have easily chosen something more upscale?—"
"Well, bluntly put, you can't really get close to the poor without living their experiences with them, without existing side by side with them."
"So by that are you dismissing charges this is little more than a photo-op, that you'll go running off to a fancy hotel in a week or so once your picture has made all the dailies, made the glossy nationals?"
"Come back next week, I'll still be here."
"Dr. King, Mayor Daley was quoted last week as saying, 'What's he doing *here,* why not let him go to Harlem.' Saying in effect, who are you, a Southerner, to come into a Northern backyard and instruct people on how to mow it. So...handed that kind of welcome in contrast to the people earlier, singing out front...."
Ffff...it stinks in here.
That's just your upper lip.
Could've sworn it was your armpit. *Snf*—yeah, that's definitely you.
Been a few months since your last bath.
I do have some memory of water.

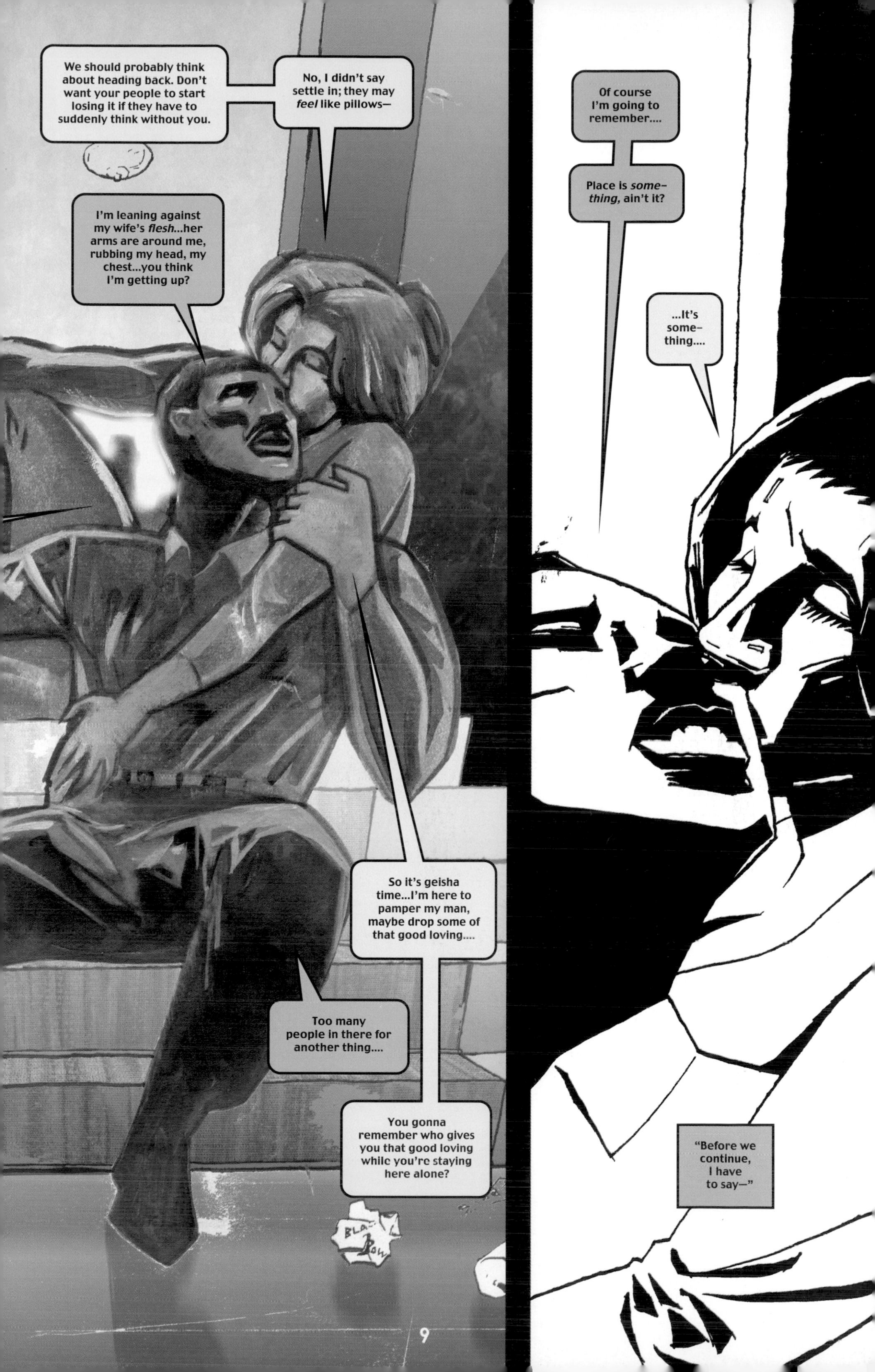
We should probably think about heading back. Don't want your people to start losing it if they have to suddenly think without you.
No, I didn't say settle in; they may *feel* like pillows—
I'm leaning against my wife's *flesh*...her arms are around me, rubbing my head, my chest...you think I'm getting up?
So it's geisha time...I'm here to pamper my man, maybe drop some of that good loving....
Too many people in there for another thing....
You gonna remember who gives you that good loving while you're staying here alone?
Of course I'm going to remember....
Place is *something,* ain't it?
...It's some-thing....
"Before we continue, I have to say—"

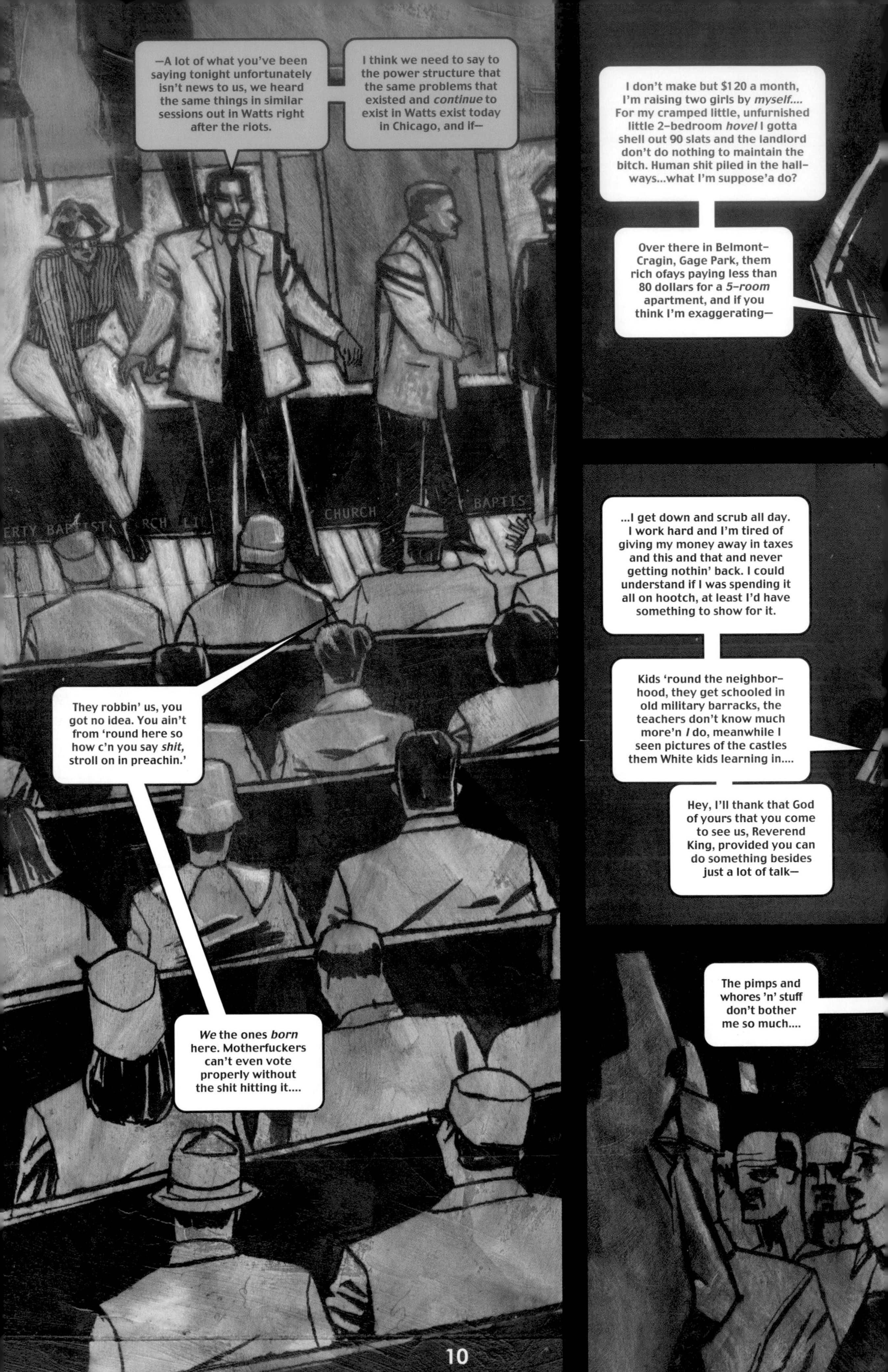
—A lot of what you've been saying tonight unfortunately isn't news to us, we heard the same things in similar sessions out in Watts right after the riots.
I think we need to say to the power structure that the same problems that existed and *continue* to exist in Watts exist today in Chicago, and if—
They robbin' us, you got no idea. You ain't from 'round here so how c'n you say *shit,* stroll on in preachin.'
We the ones *born* here. Motherfuckers can't even vote properly without the shit hitting it....
I don't make but $120 a month, I'm raising two girls by *myself....* For my cramped little, unfurnished little 2-bedroom *hovel* I gotta shell out 90 slats and the landlord don't do nothing to maintain the bitch. Human shit piled in the hallways...what I'm suppose'a do?
Over there in Belmont-Cragin, Gage Park, them rich ofays paying less than 80 dollars for a *5-room* apartment, and if you think I'm exaggerating—
...I get down and scrub all day. I work hard and I'm tired of giving my money away in taxes and this and that and never getting nothin' back. I could understand if I was spending it all on hootch, at least I'd have something to show for it.
Kids 'round the neighborhood, they get schooled in old military barracks, the teachers don't know much more'n *I* do, meanwhile I seen pictures of the castles them White kids learning in....
Hey, I'll thank that God of yours that you come to see us, Reverend King, provided you can do something besides just a lot of talk—
The pimps and whores 'n' stuff don't bother me so much....

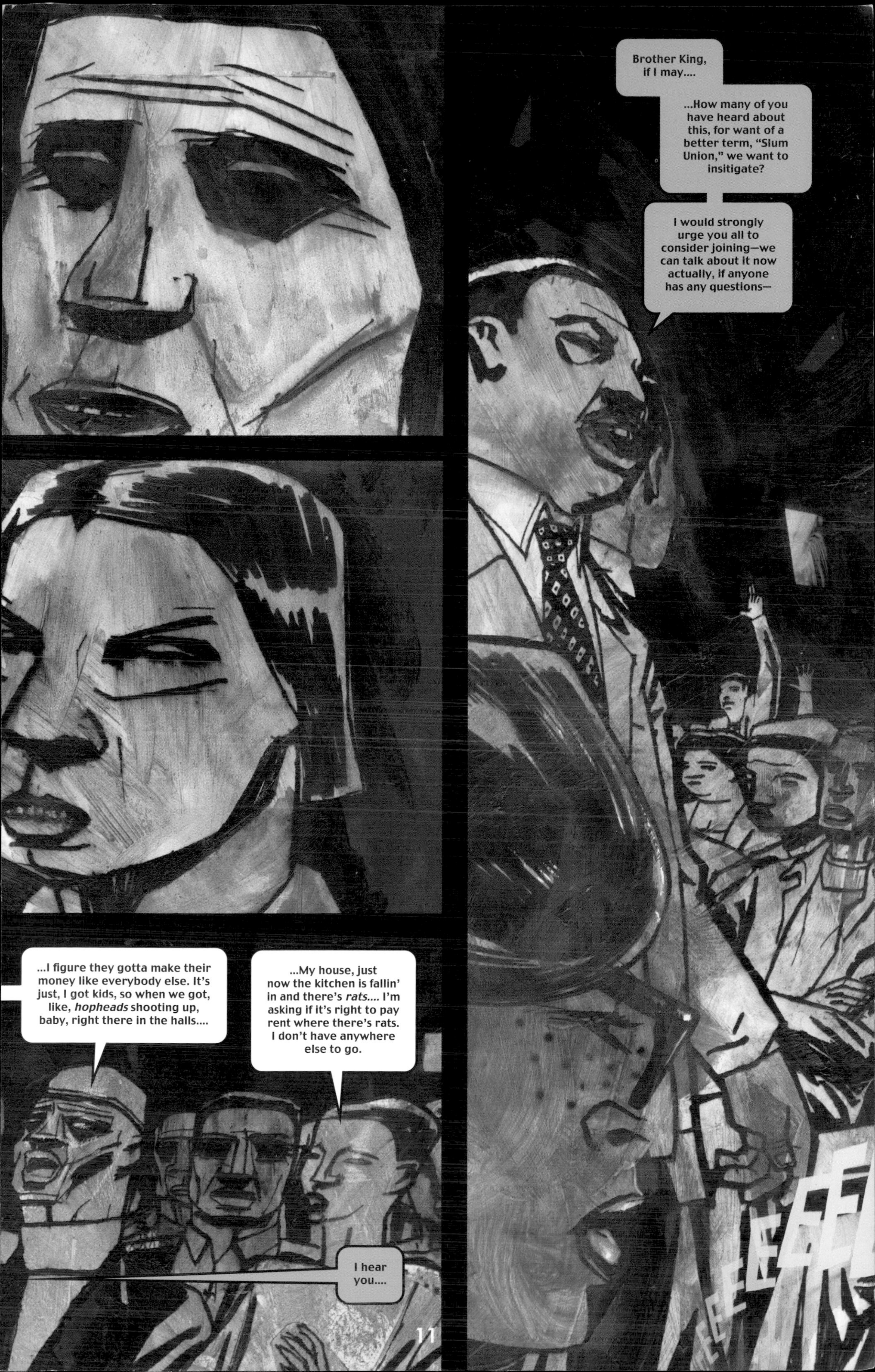
Brother King, if I may....
...How many of you have heard about this, for want of a better term, "Slum Union," we want to insitigate?
I would strongly urge you all to consider joining—we can talk about it now actually, if anyone has any questions—
...I figure they gotta make their money like everybody else. It's just, I got kids, so when we got, like, *hopheads* shooting up, baby, right there in the halls....
...My house, just now the kitchen is fallin' in and there's *rats*.... I'm asking if it's right to pay rent where there's rats. I don't have anywhere else to go.
I hear you....
EEEEEEE

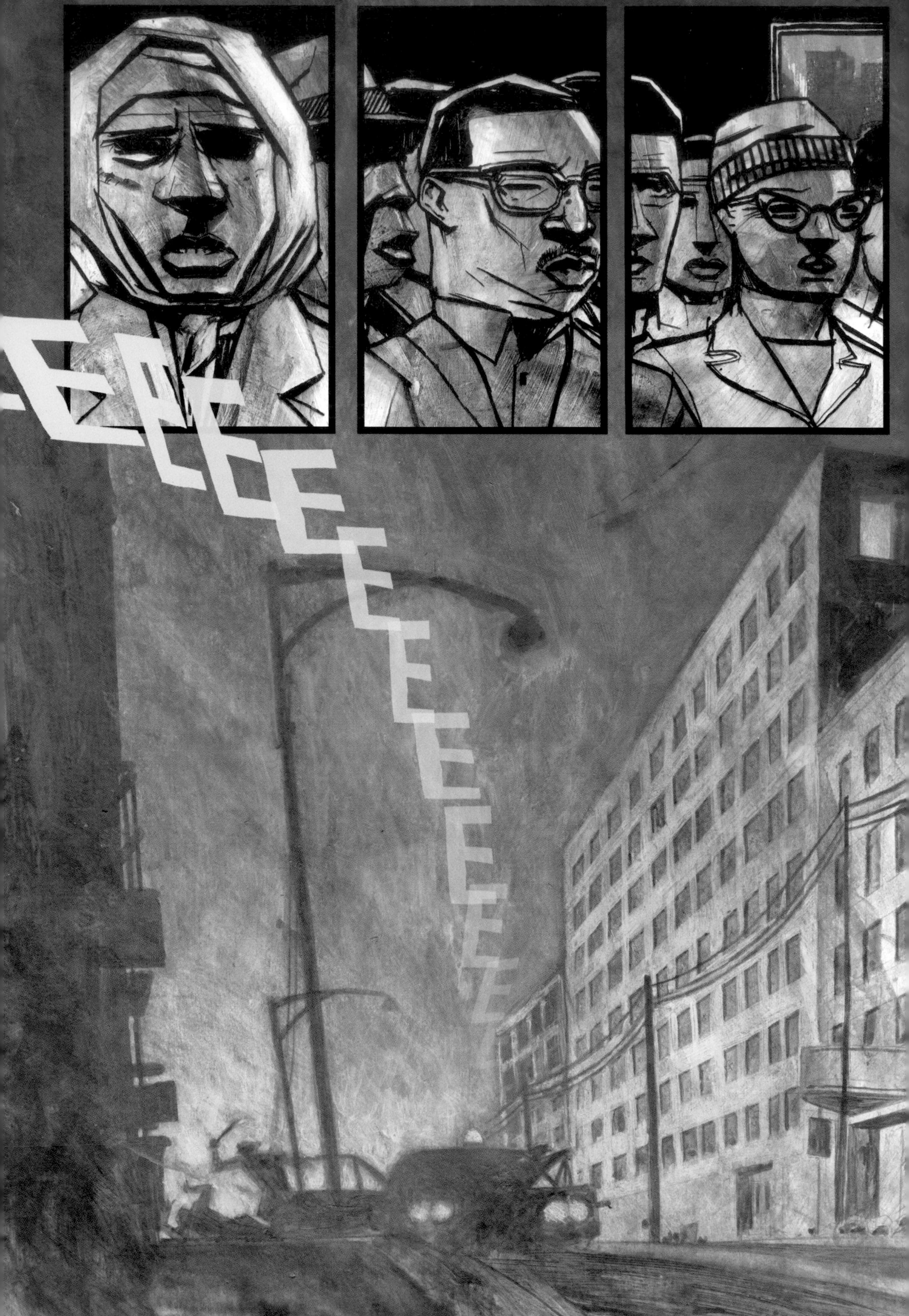
EEEEEEEEEEEEEEEE

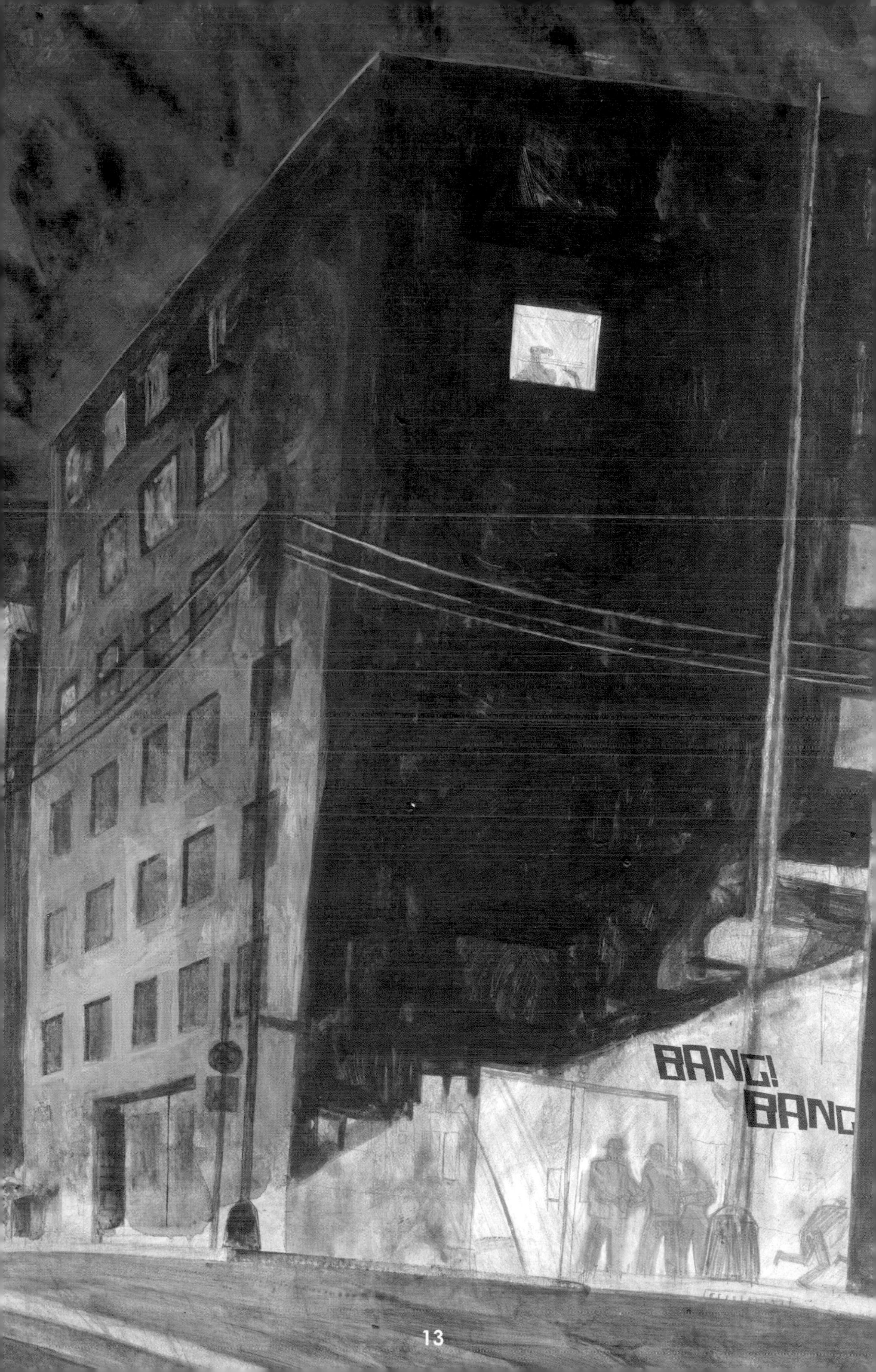
BANG!
BANG

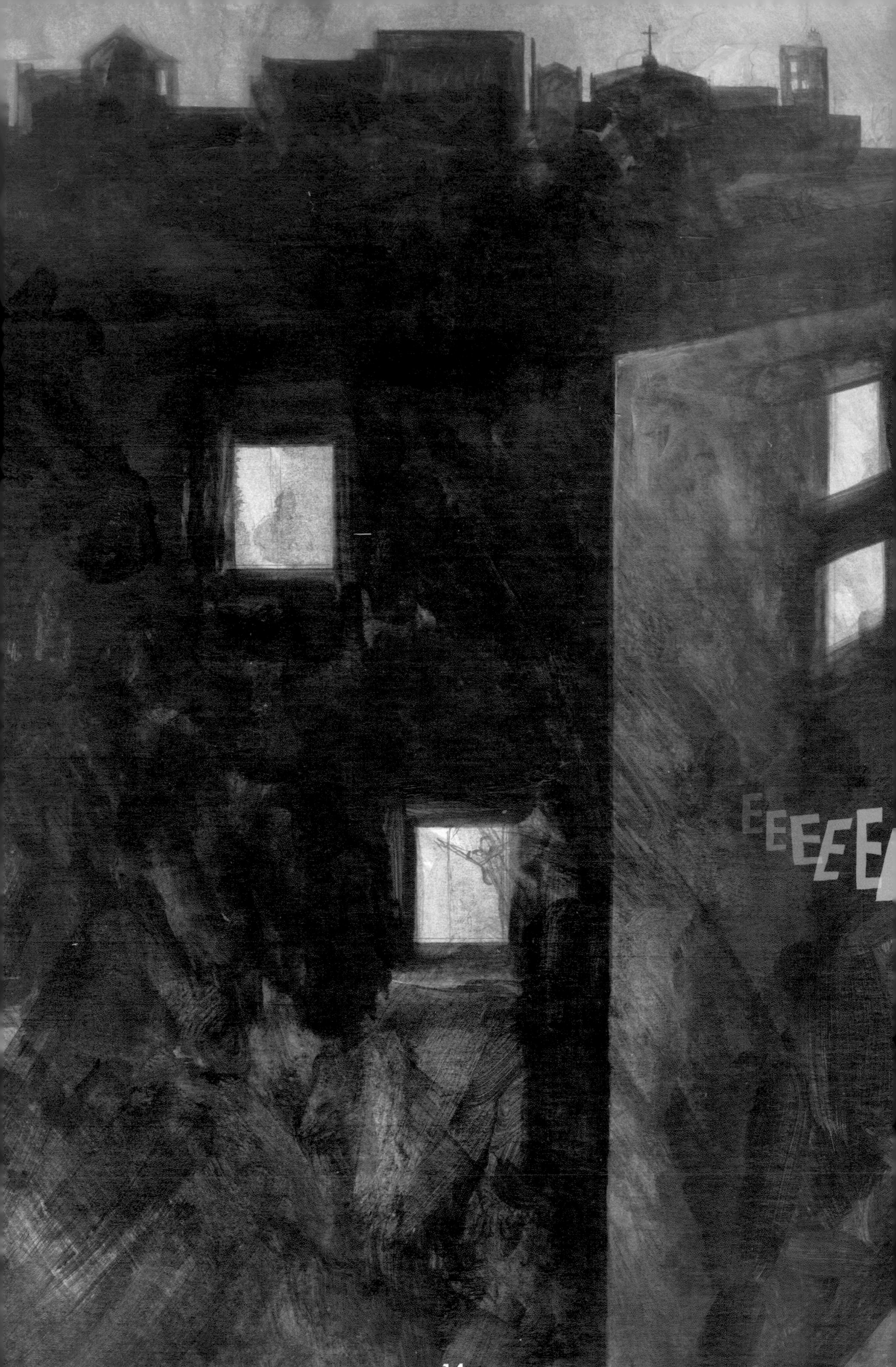
EEEEE

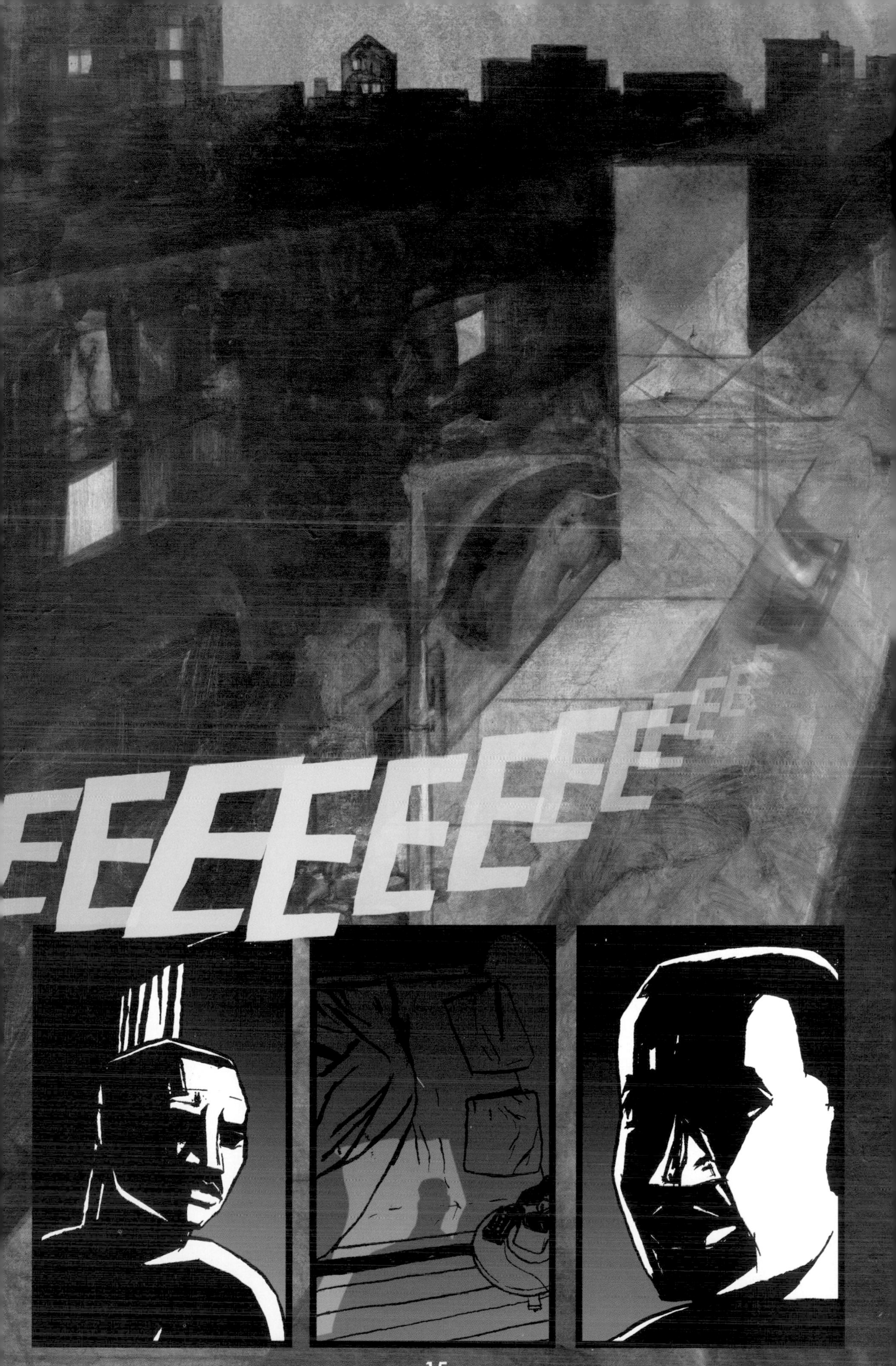
EEEEEEEEEEE

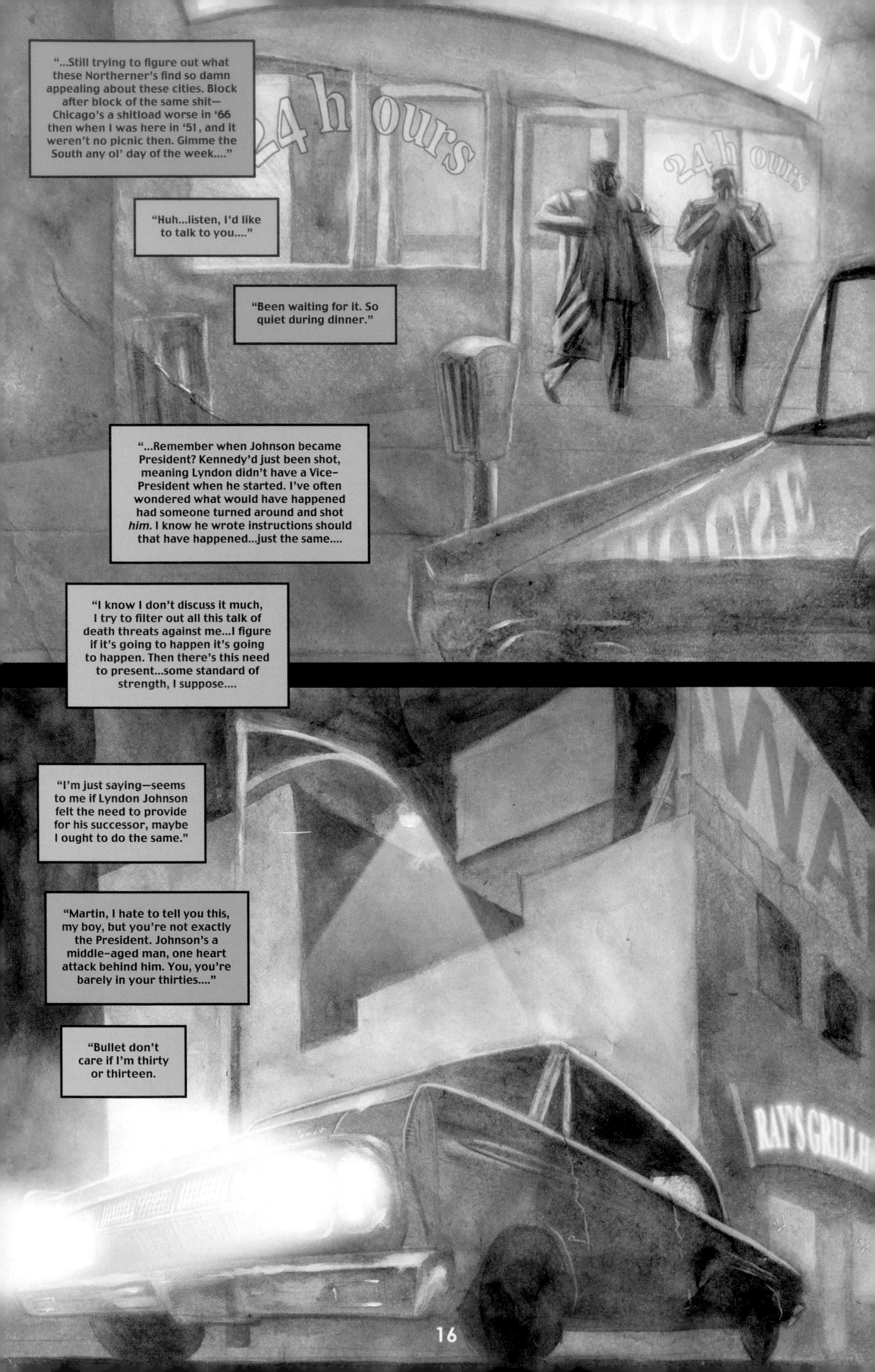
HOUSE
24 hours
24 hours
"...Still trying to figure out what these Northerner's find so damn appealing about these cities. Block after block of the same shit—Chicago's a shitload worse in '66 then when I was here in '51, and it weren't no picnic then. Gimme the South any ol' day of the week...."
"Huh...listen, I'd like to talk to you...."
"Been waiting for it. So quiet during dinner."
"...Remember when Johnson became President? Kennedy'd just been shot, meaning Lyndon didn't have a Vice-President when he started. I've often wondered what would have happened had someone turned around and shot *him.* I know he wrote instructions should that have happened...just the same....
"I know I don't discuss it much, I try to filter out all this talk of death threats against me...I figure if it's going to happen it's going to happen. Then there's this need to present...some standard of strength, I suppose....
"I'm just saying—seems to me if Lyndon Johnson felt the need to provide for his successor, maybe I ought to do the same."
"Martin, I hate to tell you this, my boy, but you're not exactly the President. Johnson's a middle-aged man, one heart attack behind him. You, you're barely in your thirties...."
"Bullet don't care if I'm thirty or thirteen.
RAY'S GRILLH

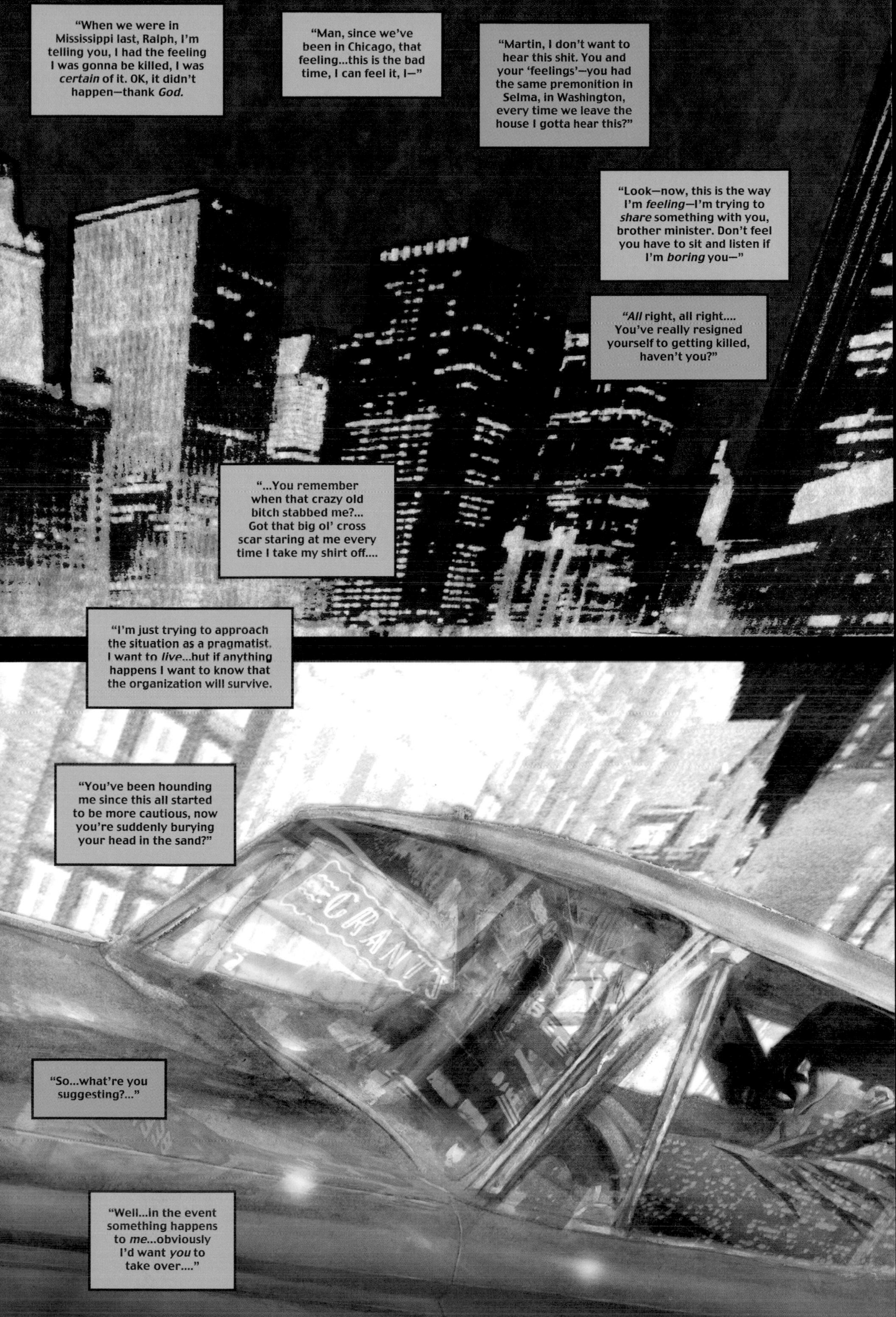
"When we were in Mississippi last, Ralph, I'm telling you, I had the feeling I was gonna be killed, I was *certain* of it. OK, it didn't happen—thank *God.*
"Man, since we've been in Chicago, that feeling...this is the bad time, I can feel it, I—"
"Martin, I don't want to hear this shit. You and your 'feelings'—you had the same premonition in Selma, in Washington, every time we leave the house I gotta hear this?"
"Look—now, this is the way I'm *feeling*—I'm trying to *share* something with you, brother minister. Don't feel you have to sit and listen if I'm *boring* you—"
"*All* right, all right.... You've really resigned yourself to getting killed, haven't you?"
"...You remember when that crazy old bitch stabbed me?... Got that big ol' cross scar staring at me every time I take my shirt off....
"I'm just trying to approach the situation as a pragmatist. I want to *live*...but if anything happens I want to know that the organization will survive.
"You've been hounding me since this all started to be more cautious, now you're suddenly burying your head in the sand?"
"So...what're you suggesting?..."
"Well...in the event something happens to *me*...obviously I'd want *you* to take over...."

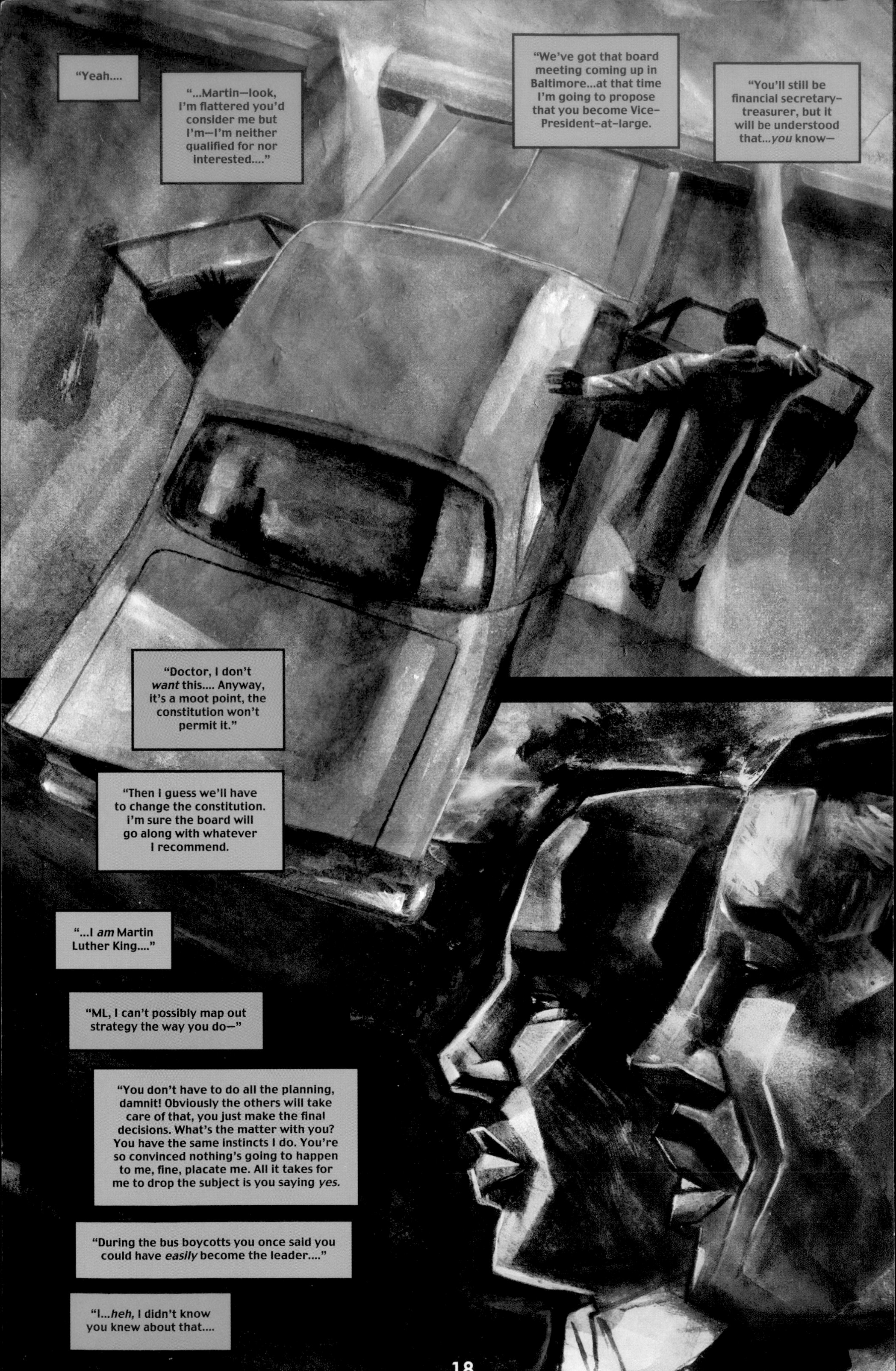
"Yeah....
"...Martin—look, I'm flattered you'd consider me but I'm—I'm neither qualified for nor interested...."
"We've got that board meeting coming up in Baltimore...at that time I'm going to propose that you become Vice-President-at-large.
"You'll still be financial secretary-treasurer, but it will be understood that...*you* know—
"Doctor, I don't *want* this.... Anyway, it's a moot point, the constitution won't permit it."
"Then I guess we'll have to change the constitution. I'm sure the board will go along with whatever I recommend.
"...I *am* Martin Luther King...."
"ML, I can't possibly map out strategy the way you do—"
"You don't have to do all the planning, damnit! Obviously the others will take care of that, you just make the final decisions. What's the matter with you? You have the same instincts I do. You're so convinced nothing's going to happen to me, fine, placate me. All it takes for me to drop the subject is you saying *yes.*
"During the bus boycotts you once said you could have *easily* become the leader...."
"I...*heh,* I didn't know you knew about that....

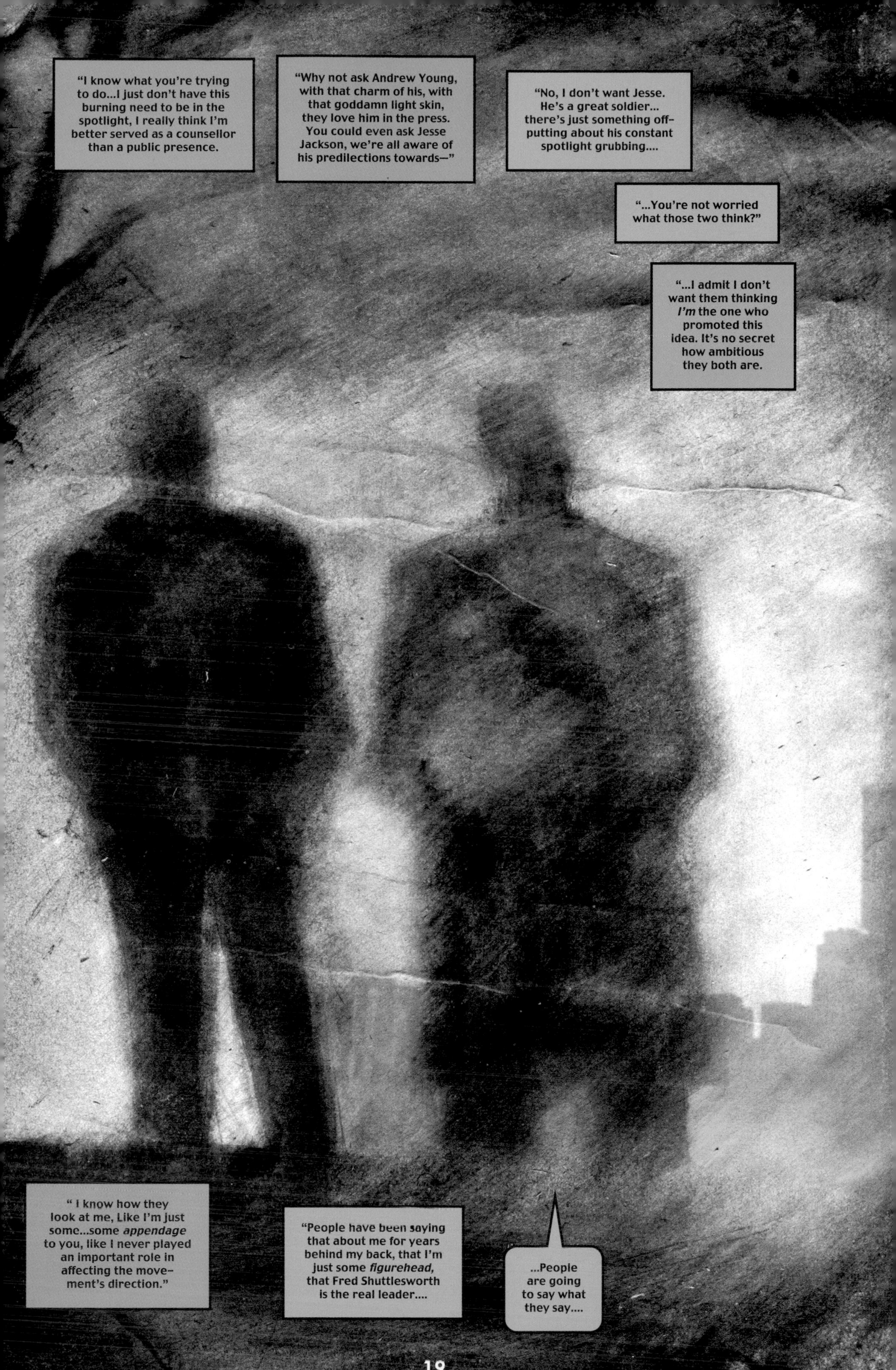
"I know what you're trying to do...I just don't have this burning need to be in the spotlight, I really think I'm better served as a counsellor than a public presence.
"Why not ask Andrew Young, with that charm of his, with that goddamn light skin, they love him in the press. You could even ask Jesse Jackson, we're all aware of his predilections towards—"
"No, I don't want Jesse. He's a great soldier... there's just something off-putting about his constant spotlight grubbing....
"...You're not worried what those two think?"
"...I admit I don't want them thinking *I'm* the one who promoted this idea. It's no secret how ambitious they both are.
" I know how they look at me, Like I'm just some...some *appendage* to you, like I never played an important role in affecting the move-ment's direction."
"People have been saying that about me for years behind my back, that I'm just some *figurehead*, that Fred Shuttlesworth is the real leader....
...People are going to say what they say....

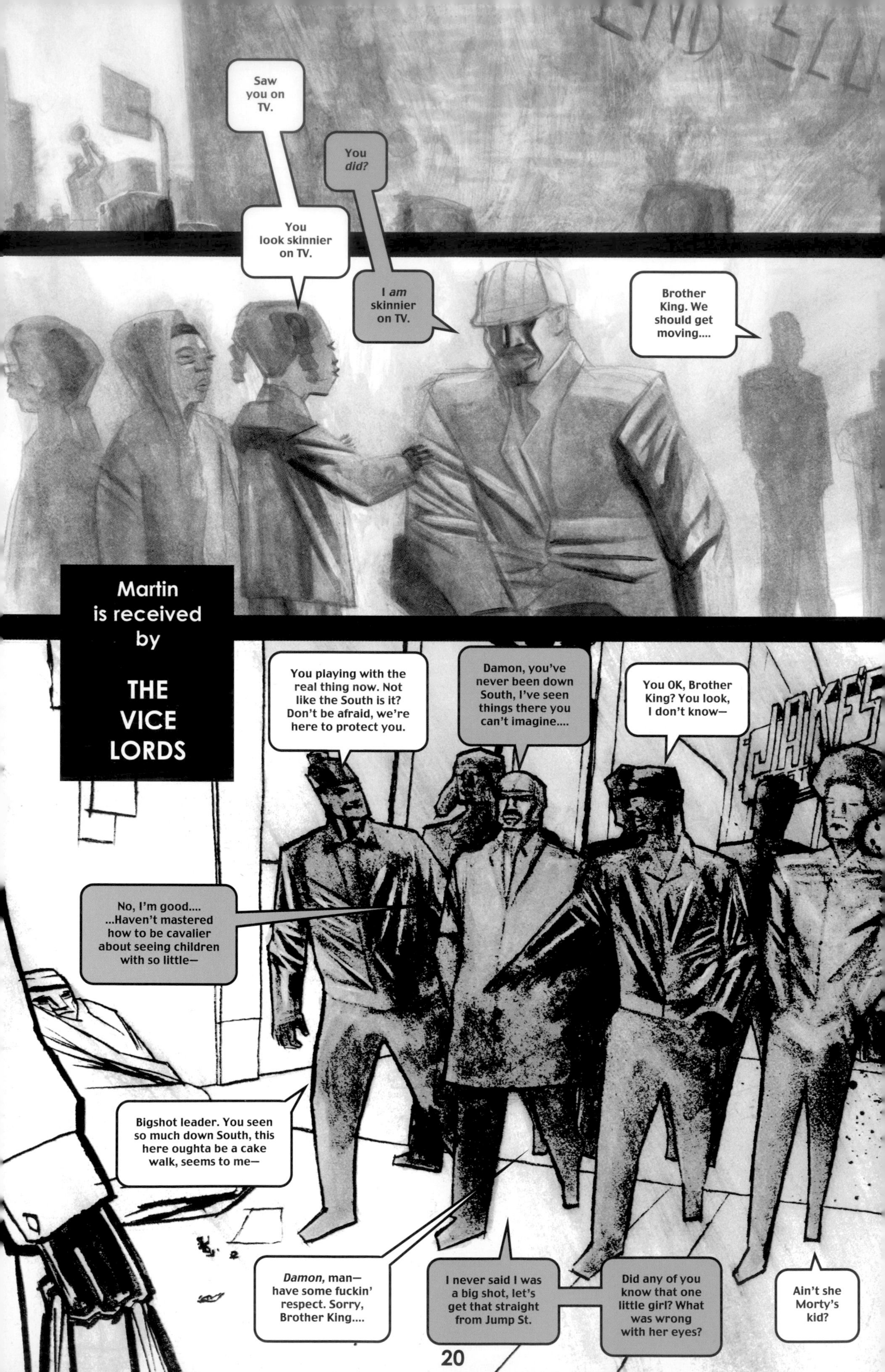

Saw you on TV.
You *did?*
You look skinnier on TV.
I *am* skinnier on TV.
Brother King. We should get moving....
Martin is received by THE VICE LORDS
You playing with the real thing now. Not like the South is it? Don't be afraid, we're here to protect you.
Damon, you've never been down South, I've seen things there you can't imagine....
You OK, Brother King? You look, I don't know—
No, I'm good.... ...Haven't mastered how to be cavalier about seeing children with so little—
Bigshot leader. You seen so much down South, this here oughta be a cake walk, seems to me—
Damon, man— have some fuckin' respect. Sorry, Brother King....
I never said I was a big shot, let's get that straight from Jump St.
Did any of you know that one little girl? What was wrong with her eyes?
Ain't she Morty's kid?

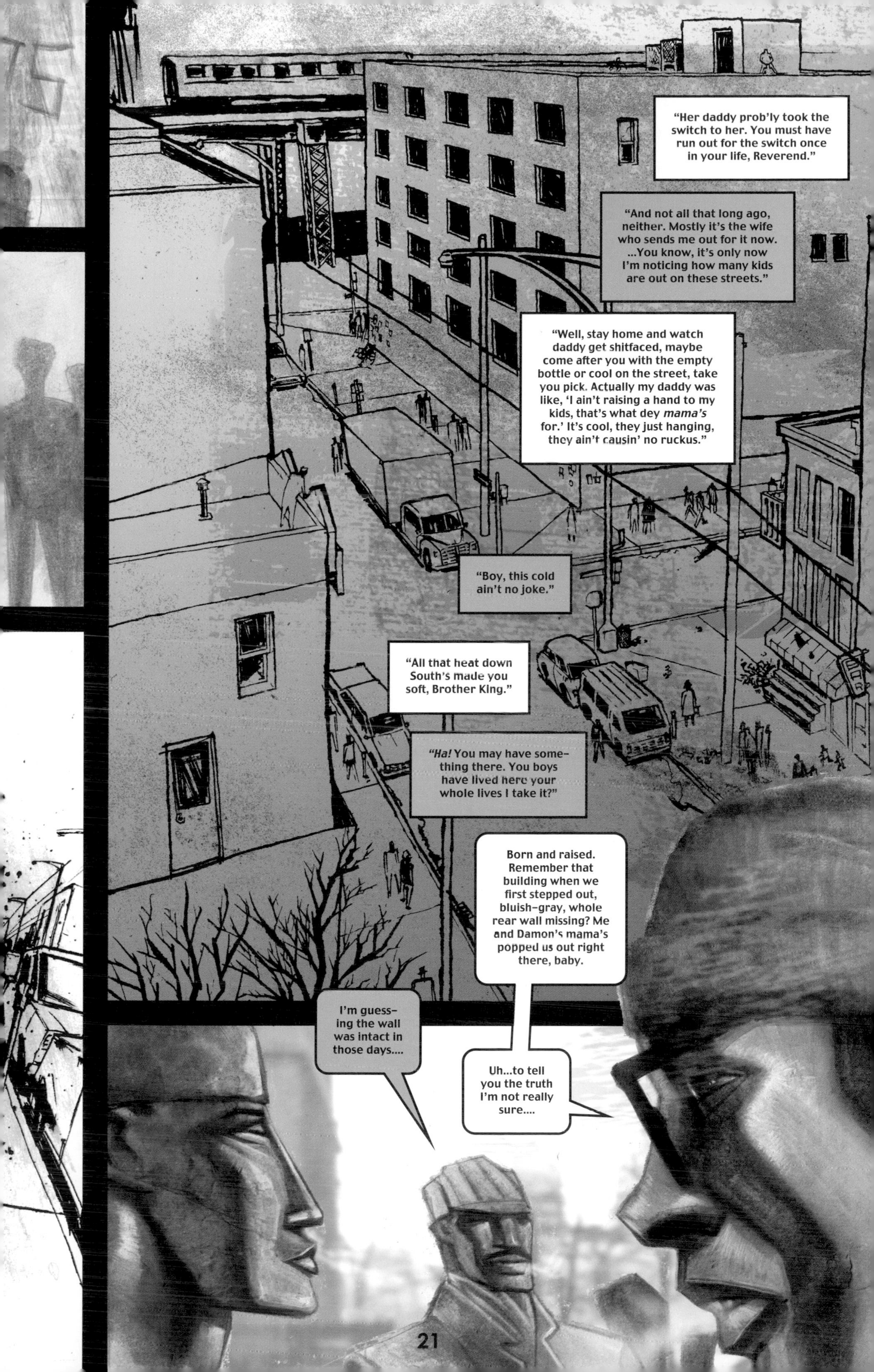
"Her daddy prob'ly took the switch to her. You must have run out for the switch once in your life, Reverend."
"And not all that long ago, neither. Mostly it's the wife who sends me out for it now. ...You know, it's only now I'm noticing how many kids are out on these streets."
"Well, stay home and watch daddy get shitfaced, maybe come after you with the empty bottle or cool on the street, take you pick. Actually my daddy was like, 'I ain't raising a hand to my kids, that's what dey *mama's* for.' It's cool, they just hanging, they ain't causin' no ruckus."
"Boy, this cold ain't no joke."
"All that heat down South's made you soft, Brother King."
"*Ha!* You may have some-thing there. You boys have lived here your whole lives I take it?"
Born and raised. Remember that building when we first stepped out, bluish-gray, whole rear wall missing? Me and Damon's mama's popped us out right there, baby.
I'm guess-ing the wall was intact in those days....
Uh...to tell you the truth I'm not really sure....

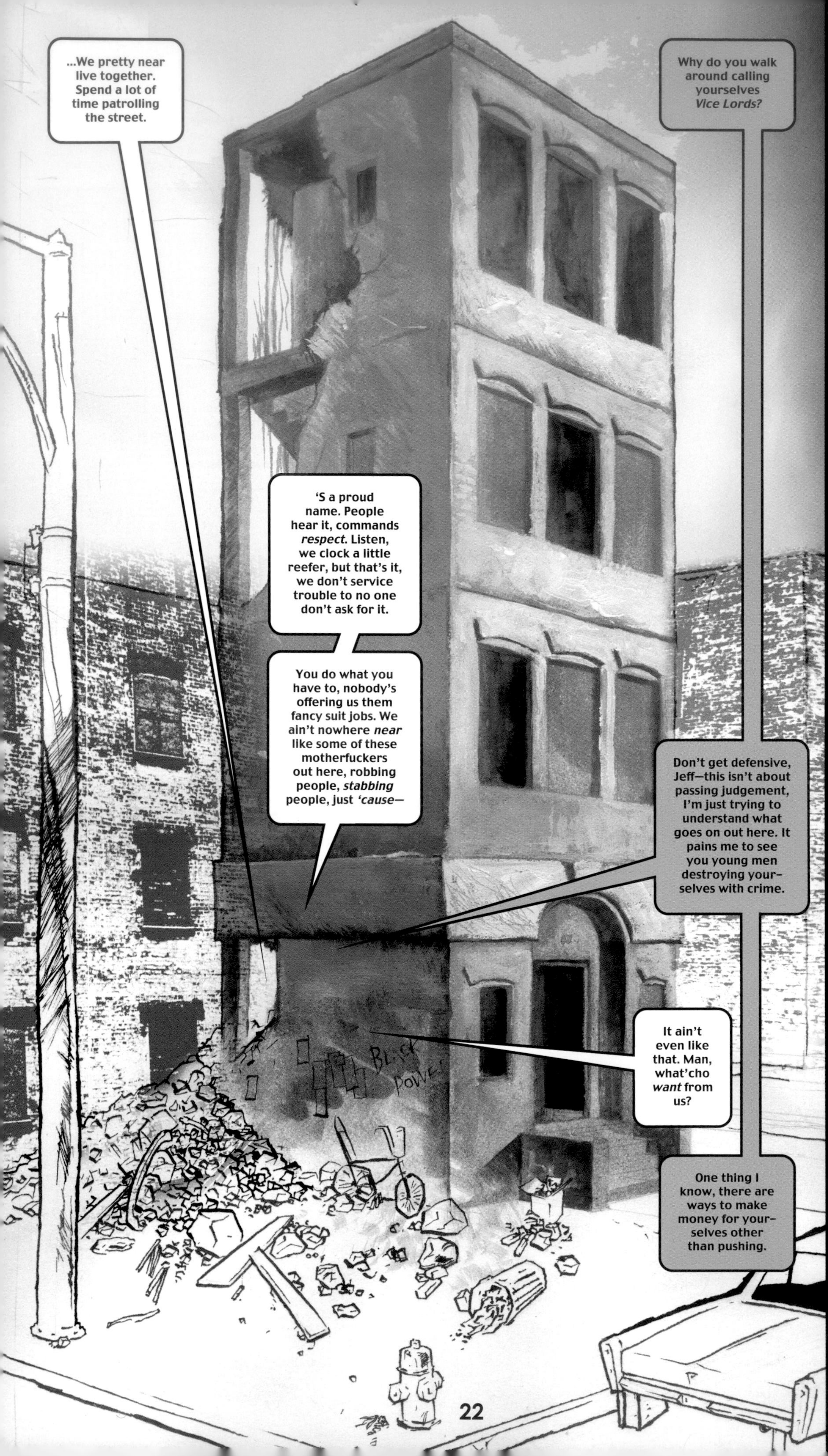
...We pretty near live together. Spend a lot of time patrolling the street.
Why do you walk around calling yourselves *Vice Lords?*
'S a proud name. People hear it, commands *respect.* Listen, we clock a little reefer, but that's it, we don't service trouble to no one don't ask for it.
You do what you have to, nobody's offering us them fancy suit jobs. We ain't nowhere *near* like some of these motherfuckers out here, robbing people, *stabbing* people, just *'cause—*
Don't get defensive, Jeff—this isn't about passing judgement, I'm just trying to understand what goes on out here. It pains me to see you young men destroying your-selves with crime.
It ain't even like that. Man, what'cho *want* from us?
One thing I know, there are ways to make money for your-selves other than pushing.
BLACK POWE

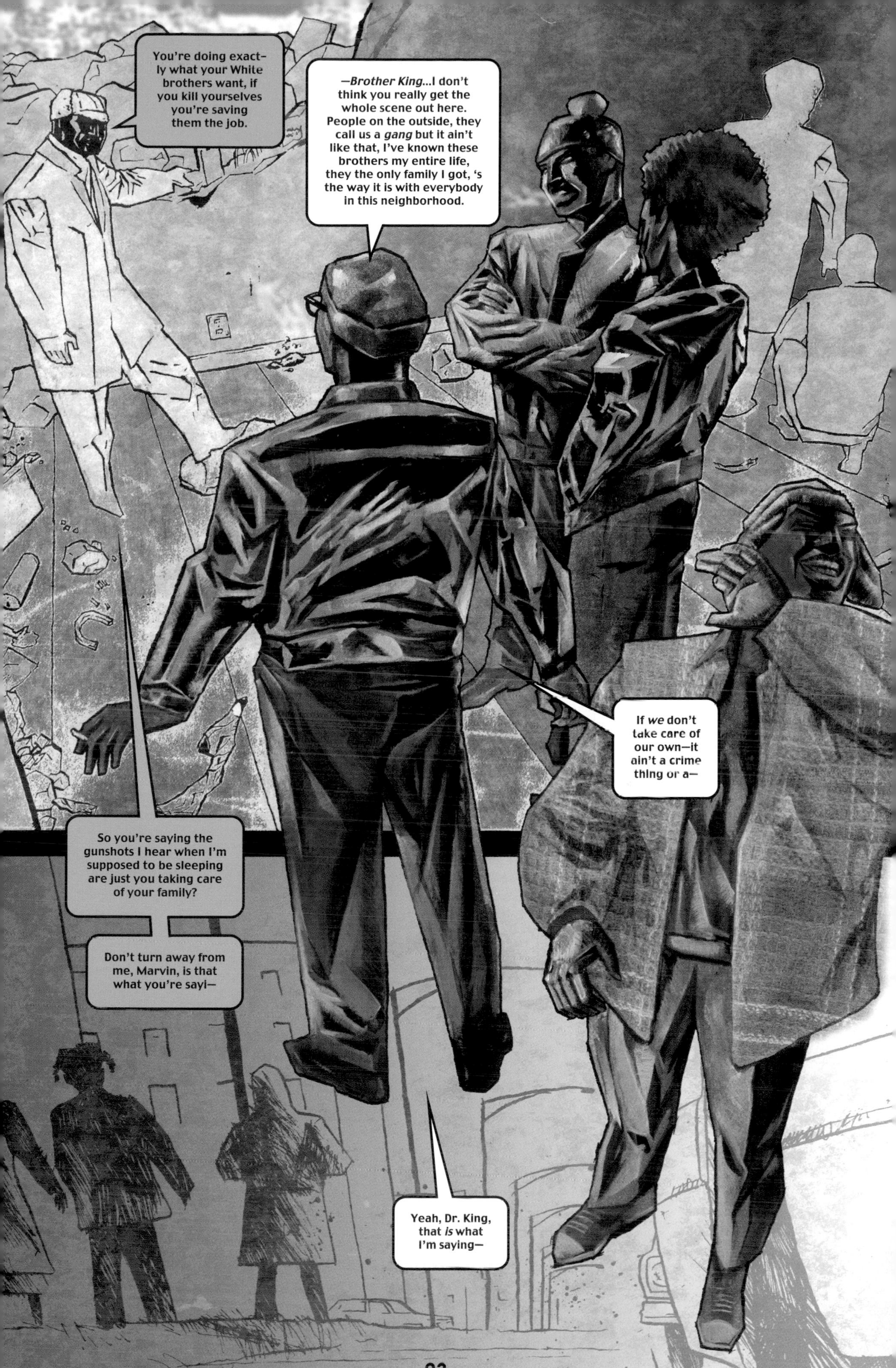

You're doing exactly what your White brothers want, if you kill yourselves you're saving them the job.
—*Brother King*...I don't think you really get the whole scene out here. People on the outside, they call us a *gang* but it ain't like that, I've known these brothers my entire life, they the only family I got, 's the way it is with everybody in this neighborhood.
If *we* don't take care of our own—it ain't a crime thing or a—
So you're saying the gunshots I hear when I'm supposed to be sleeping are just you taking care of your family?
Don't turn away from me, Marvin, is that what you're sayi—
Yeah, Dr. King, that *is* what I'm saying—

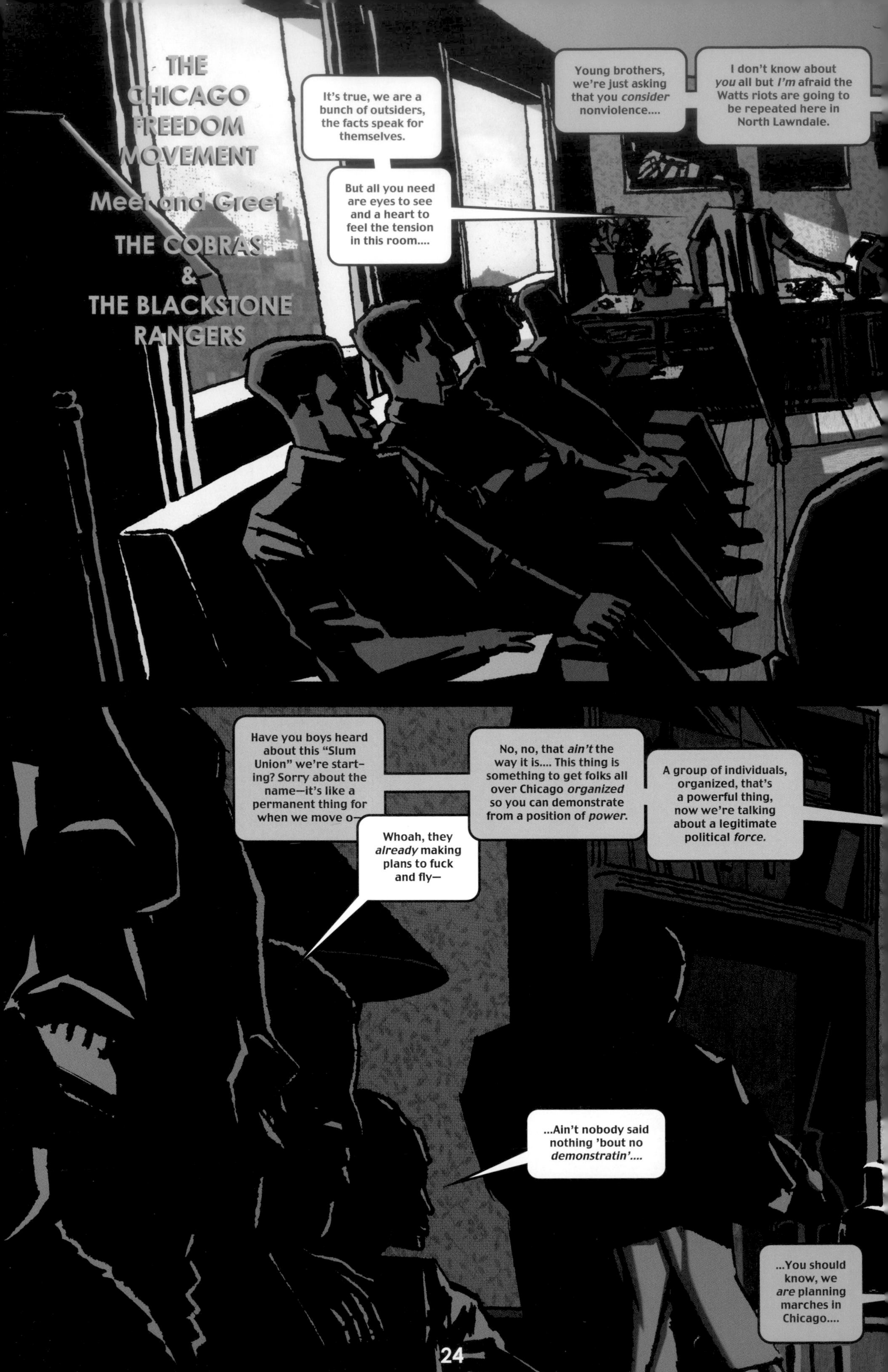
THE CHICAGO FREEDOM MOVEMENT
Meet and Greet
THE COBRAS & THE BLACKSTONE RANGERS
It's true, we are a bunch of outsiders, the facts speak for themselves.
But all you need are eyes to see and a heart to feel the tension in this room....
Young brothers, we're just asking that you *consider* nonviolence....
I don't know about *you* all but *I'm* afraid the Watts riots are going to be repeated here in North Lawndale.
Have you boys heard about this "Slum Union" we're start-ing? Sorry about the name—it's like a permanent thing for when we move o—
Whoah, they *already* making plans to fuck and fly—
No, no, that *ain't* the way it is.... This thing is something to get folks all over Chicago *organized* so you can demonstrate from a position of *power.*
A group of individuals, organized, that's a powerful thing, now we're talking about a legitimate political *force.*
...Ain't nobody said nothing 'bout no *demonstratin'*....
...You should know, we *are* planning marches in Chicago....

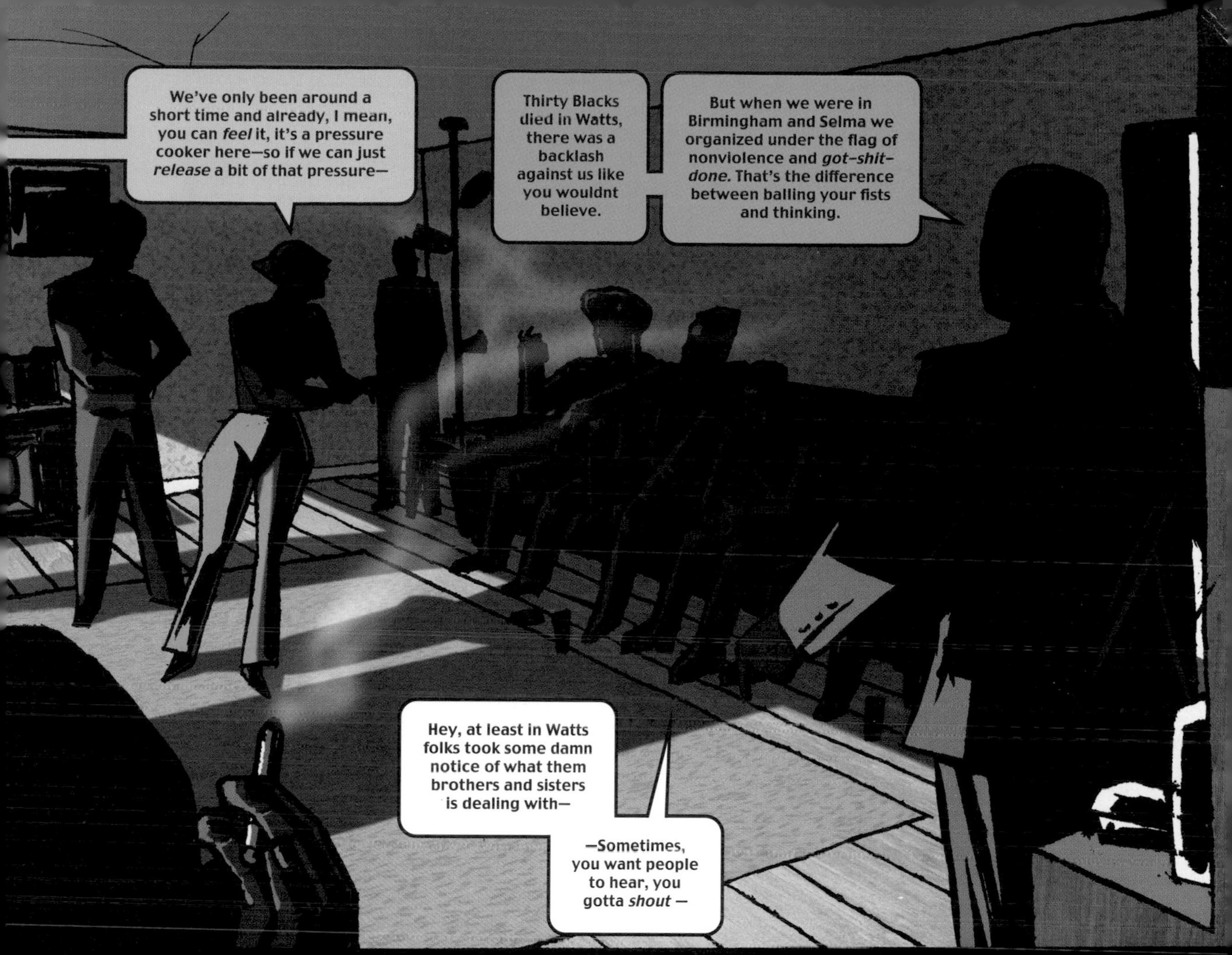
We've only been around a short time and already, I mean, you can *feel* it, it's a pressure cooker here—so if we can just *release* a bit of that pressure—
Thirty Blacks died in Watts, there was a backlash against us like you wouldnt believe.
But when we were in Birmingham and Selma we organized under the flag of nonviolence and *got-shit-done.* That's the difference between balling your fists and thinking.
Hey, at least in Watts folks took some damn notice of what them brothers and sisters is dealing with—
—Sometimes, you want people to hear, you gotta *shout* —

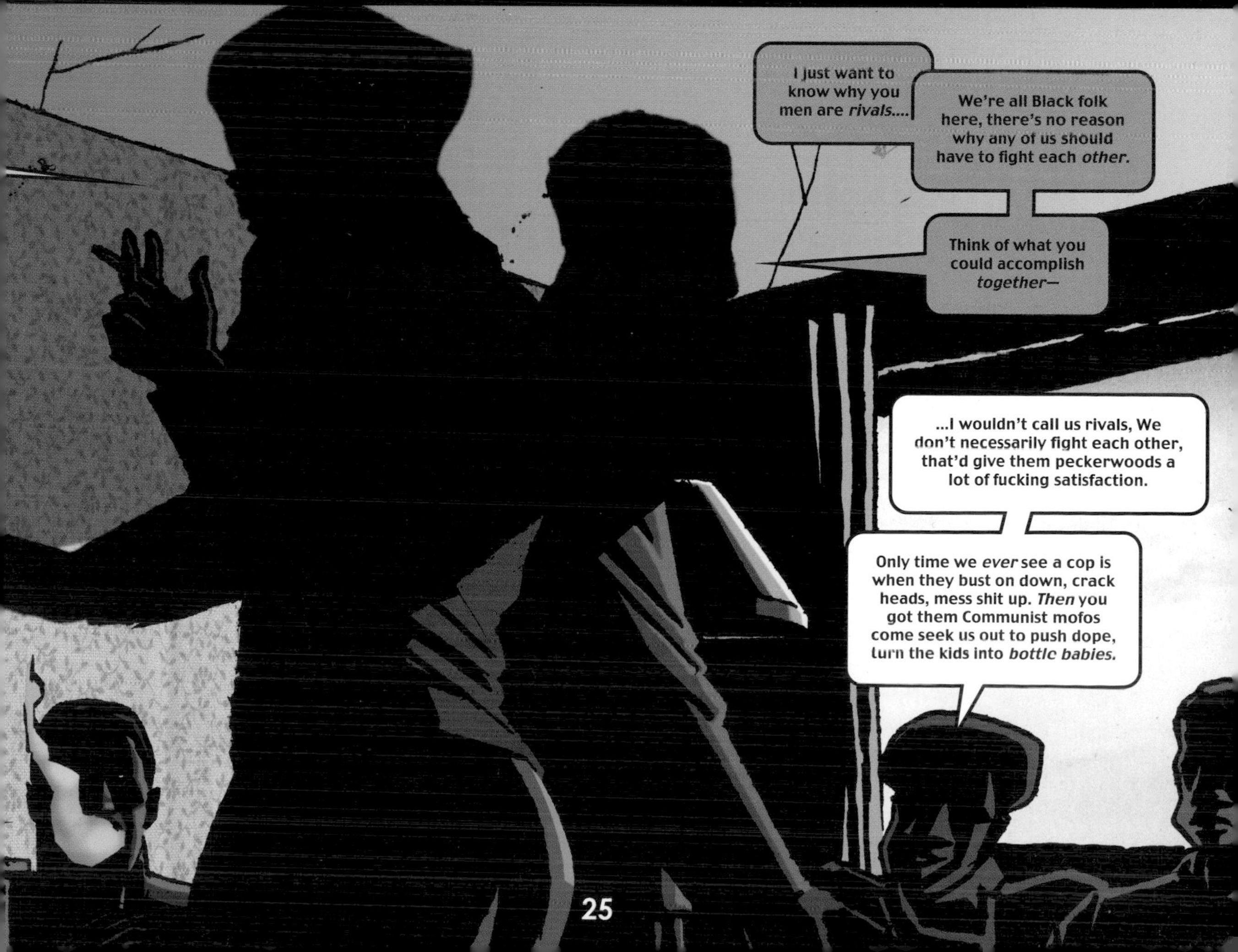
I just want to know why you men are *rivals....*
We're all Black folk here, there's no reason why any of us should have to fight each *other.*
Think of what you could accomplish *together*—
...I wouldn't call us rivals, We don't necessarily fight each other, that'd give them peckerwoods a lot of fucking satisfaction.
Only time we *ever* see a cop is when they bust on down, crack heads, mess shit up. *Then* you got them Communist mofos come seek us out to push dope, turn the kids into *bottle babies.*

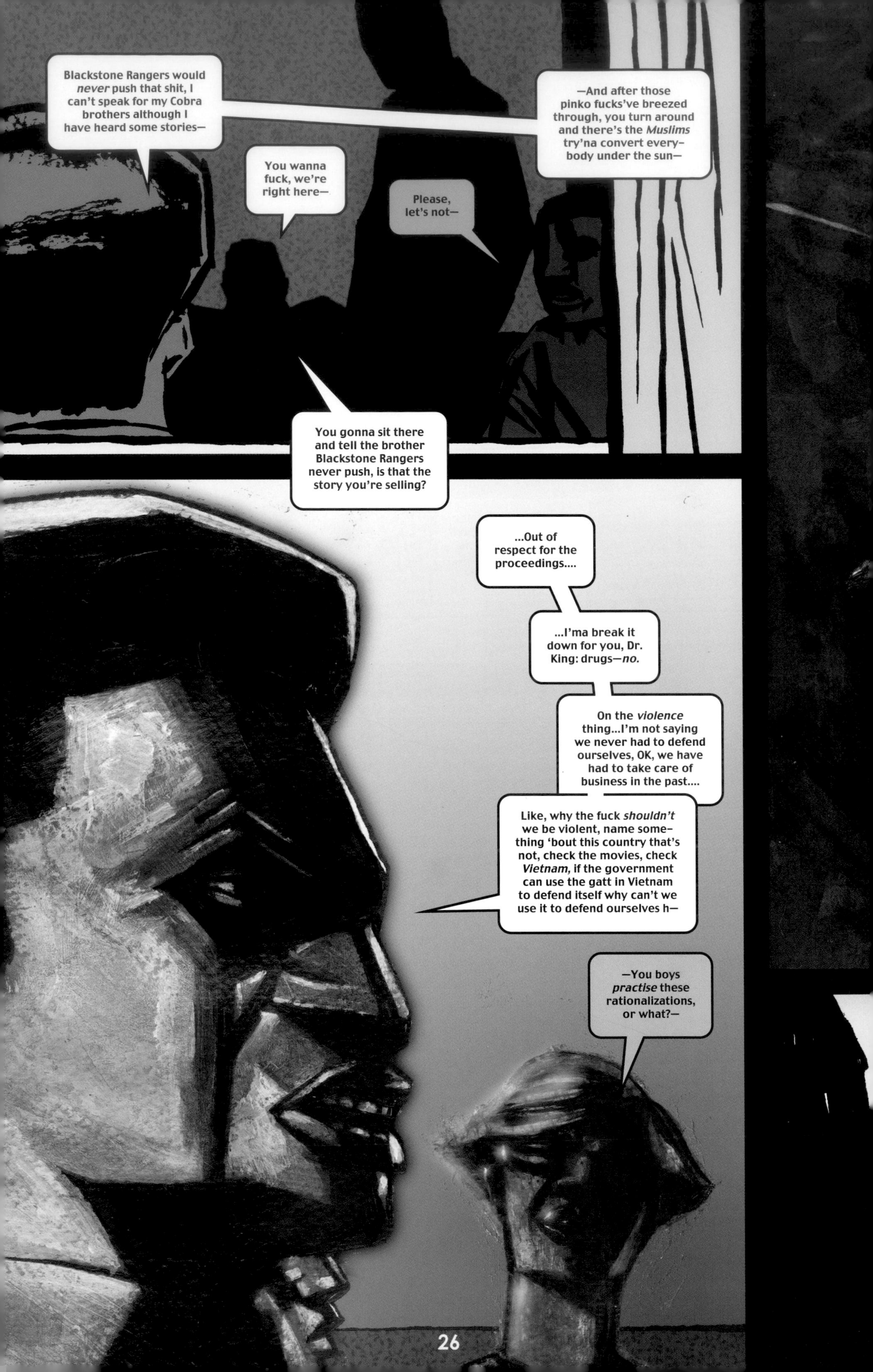
Blackstone Rangers would *never* push that shit, I can't speak for my Cobra brothers although I have heard some stories—
—And after those pinko fucks've breezed through, you turn around and there's the *Muslims* try'na convert every-body under the sun—
You wanna fuck, we're right here—
Please, let's not—
You gonna sit there and tell the brother Blackstone Rangers never push, is that the story you're selling?
...Out of respect for the proceedings....
...I'ma break it down for you, Dr. King: drugs—*no.*
On the *violence* thing...I'm not saying we never had to defend ourselves, OK, we have had to take care of business in the past....
Like, why the fuck *shouldn't* we be violent, name some-thing 'bout this country that's not, check the movies, check *Vietnam,* if the government can use the gatt in Vietnam to defend itself why can't we use it to defend ourselves h—
—You boys *practise* these rationalizations, or what?—

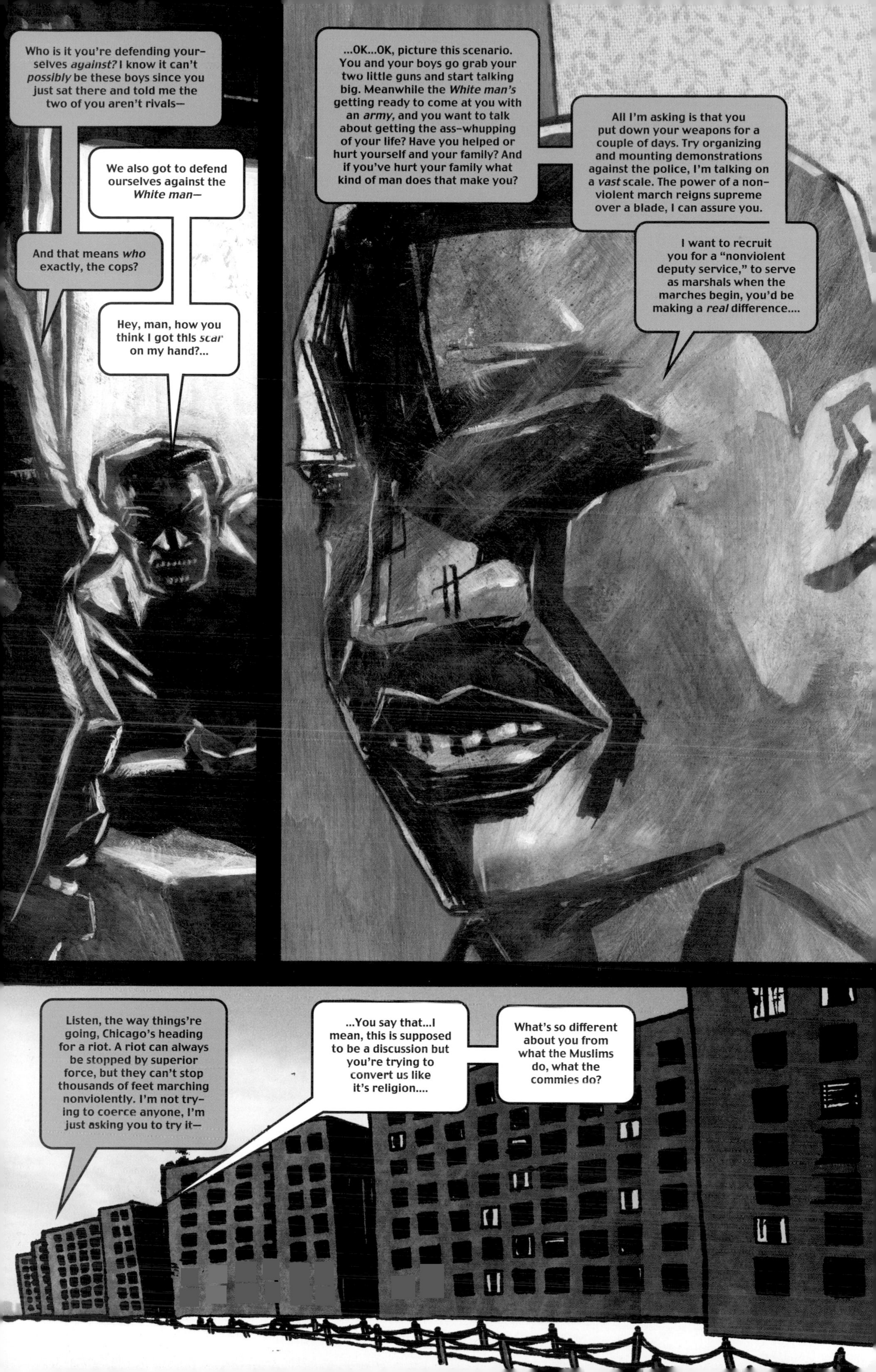
Who is it you're defending yourselves *against?* I know it can't *possibly* be these boys since you just sat there and told me the two of you aren't rivals—
We also got to defend ourselves against the *White man*—
And that means *who* exactly, the cops?
Hey, man, how you think I got this *scar* on my hand?...
...OK...OK, picture this scenario. You and your boys go grab your two little guns and start talking big. Meanwhile the *White man's* getting ready to come at you with an *army,* and you want to talk about getting the ass-whupping of your life? Have you helped or hurt yourself and your family? And if you've hurt your family what kind of man does that make you?
All I'm asking is that you put down your weapons for a couple of days. Try organizing and mounting demonstrations against the police, I'm talking on a *vast* scale. The power of a nonviolent march reigns supreme over a blade, I can assure you.
I want to recruit you for a "nonviolent deputy service," to serve as marshals when the marches begin, you'd be making a *real* difference....
Listen, the way things're going, Chicago's heading for a riot. A riot can always be stopped by superior force, but they can't stop thousands of feet marching nonviolently. I'm not trying to coerce anyone, I'm just asking you to try it—
...You say that...I mean, this is supposed to be a discussion but you're trying to convert us like it's religion....
What's so different about you from what the Muslims do, what the commies do?

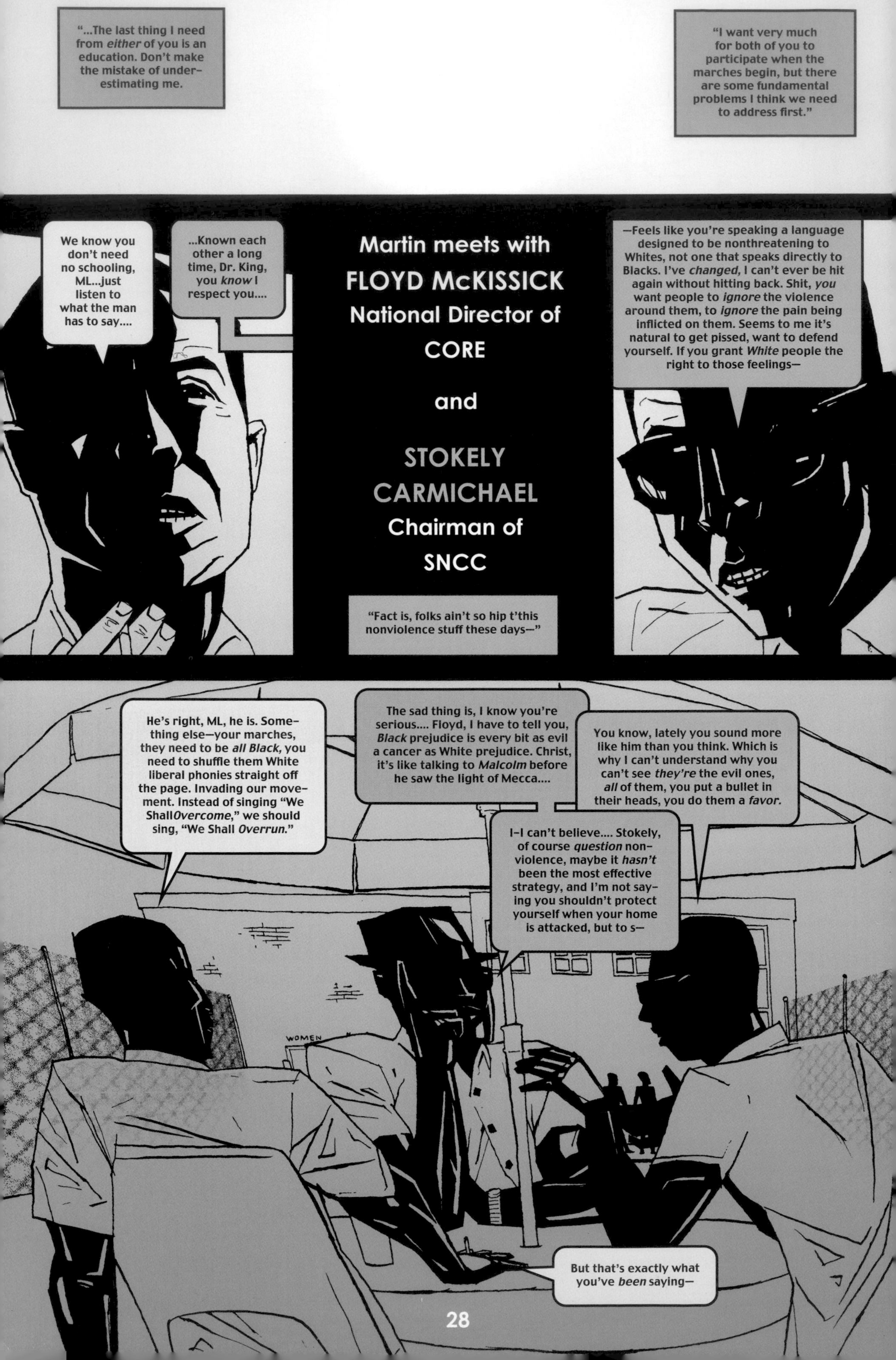
"...The last thing I need from *either* of you is an education. Don't make the mistake of under-estimating me.
"I want very much for both of you to participate when the marches begin, but there are some fundamental problems I think we need to address first."
We know you don't need no schooling, ML...just listen to what the man has to say....
...Known each other a long time, Dr. King, you *know* I respect you....
Martin meets with FLOYD McKISSICK National Director of CORE and STOKELY CARMICHAEL Chairman of SNCC
"Fact is, folks ain't so hip t'this nonviolence stuff these days—"
—Feels like you're speaking a language designed to be nonthreatening to Whites, not one that speaks directly to Blacks. I've *changed,* I can't ever be hit again without hitting back. Shit, *you* want people to *ignore* the violence around them, to *ignore* the pain being inflicted on them. Seems to me it's natural to get pissed, want to defend yourself. If you grant *White* people the right to those feelings—
He's right, ML, he is. Something else—your marches, they need to be *all Black,* you need to shuffle them White liberal phonies straight off the page. Invading our movement. Instead of singing "We Shall *Overcome,*" we should sing, "We Shall *Overrun.*"
The sad thing is, I know you're serious.... Floyd, I have to tell you, *Black* prejudice is every bit as evil a cancer as White prejudice. Christ, it's like talking to *Malcolm* before he saw the light of Mecca....
You know, lately you sound more like him than you think. Which is why I can't understand why you can't see *they're* the evil ones, *all* of them, you put a bullet in their heads, you do them a *favor.*
I-I can't believe.... Stokely, of course *question* non-violence, maybe it *hasn't* been the most effective strategy, and I'm not saying you shouldn't protect yourself when your home is attacked, but to s—
WOMEN
But that's exactly what you've *been* saying—

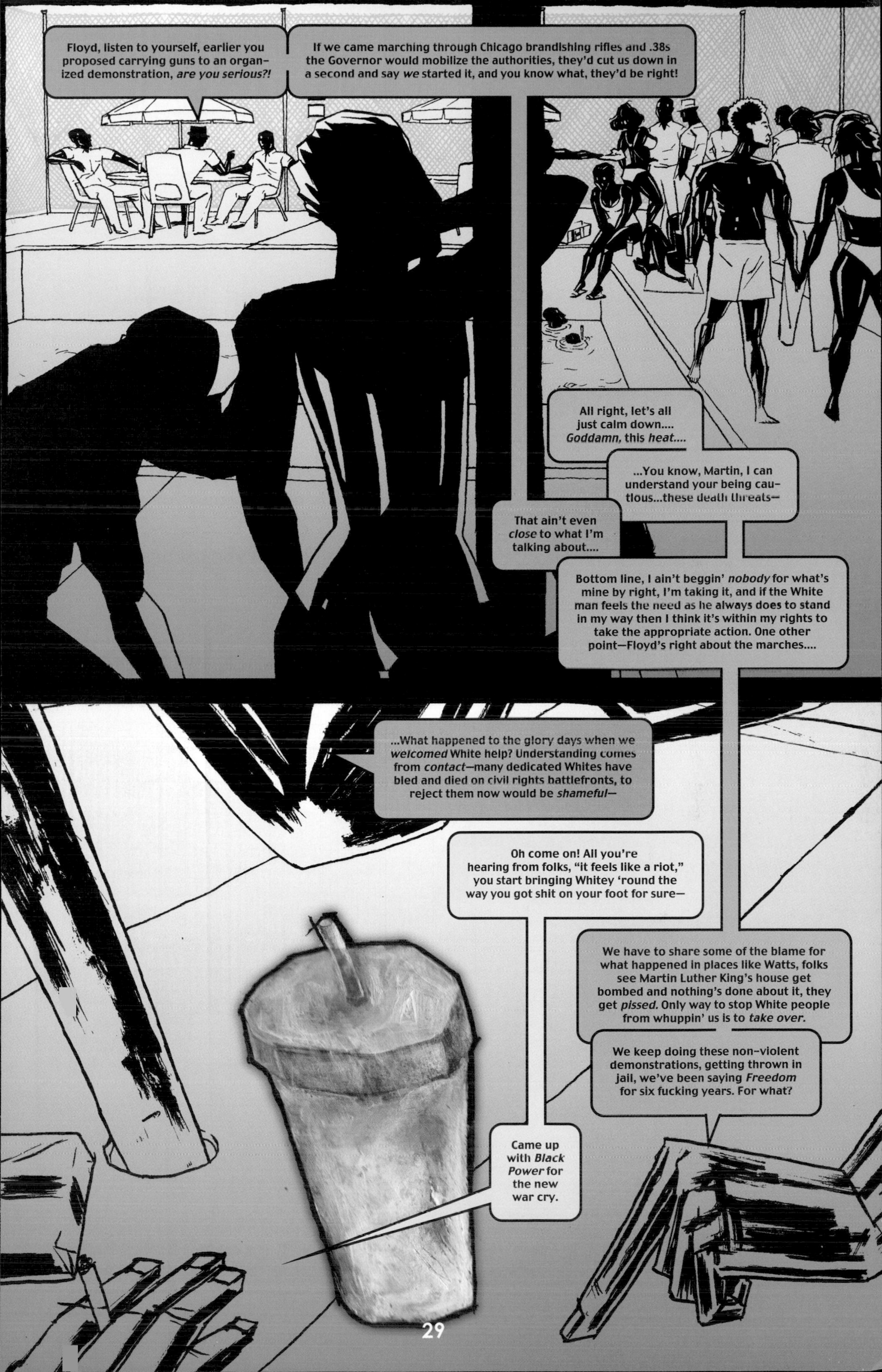

Floyd, listen to yourself, earlier you proposed carrying guns to an organ-ized demonstration, *are you serious?!*
If we came marching through Chicago brandishing rifles and .38s the Governor would mobilize the authorities, they'd cut us down in a second and say *we* started it, and you know what, they'd be right!
All right, let's all just calm down.... *Goddamn,* this *heat....*
...You know, Martin, I can understand your being cau-tious...these death threats—
That ain't even *close* to what I'm talking about....
Bottom line, I ain't beggin' *nobody* for what's mine by right, I'm taking it, and if the White man feels the need as he always does to stand in my way then I think it's within my rights to take the appropriate action. One other point—Floyd's right about the marches....
...What happened to the glory days when we *welcomed* White help? Understanding comes from *contact*—many dedicated Whites have bled and died on civil rights battlefronts, to reject them now would be *shameful*—
Oh come on! All you're hearing from folks, "it feels like a riot," you start bringing Whitey 'round the way you got shit on your foot for sure—
We have to share some of the blame for what happened in places like Watts, folks see Martin Luther King's house get bombed and nothing's done about it, they get *pissed.* Only way to stop White people from whuppin' us is to *take over.*
We keep doing these non-violent demonstrations, getting thrown in jail, we've been saying *Freedom* for six fucking years. For what?
Came up with *Black Power* for the new war cry.

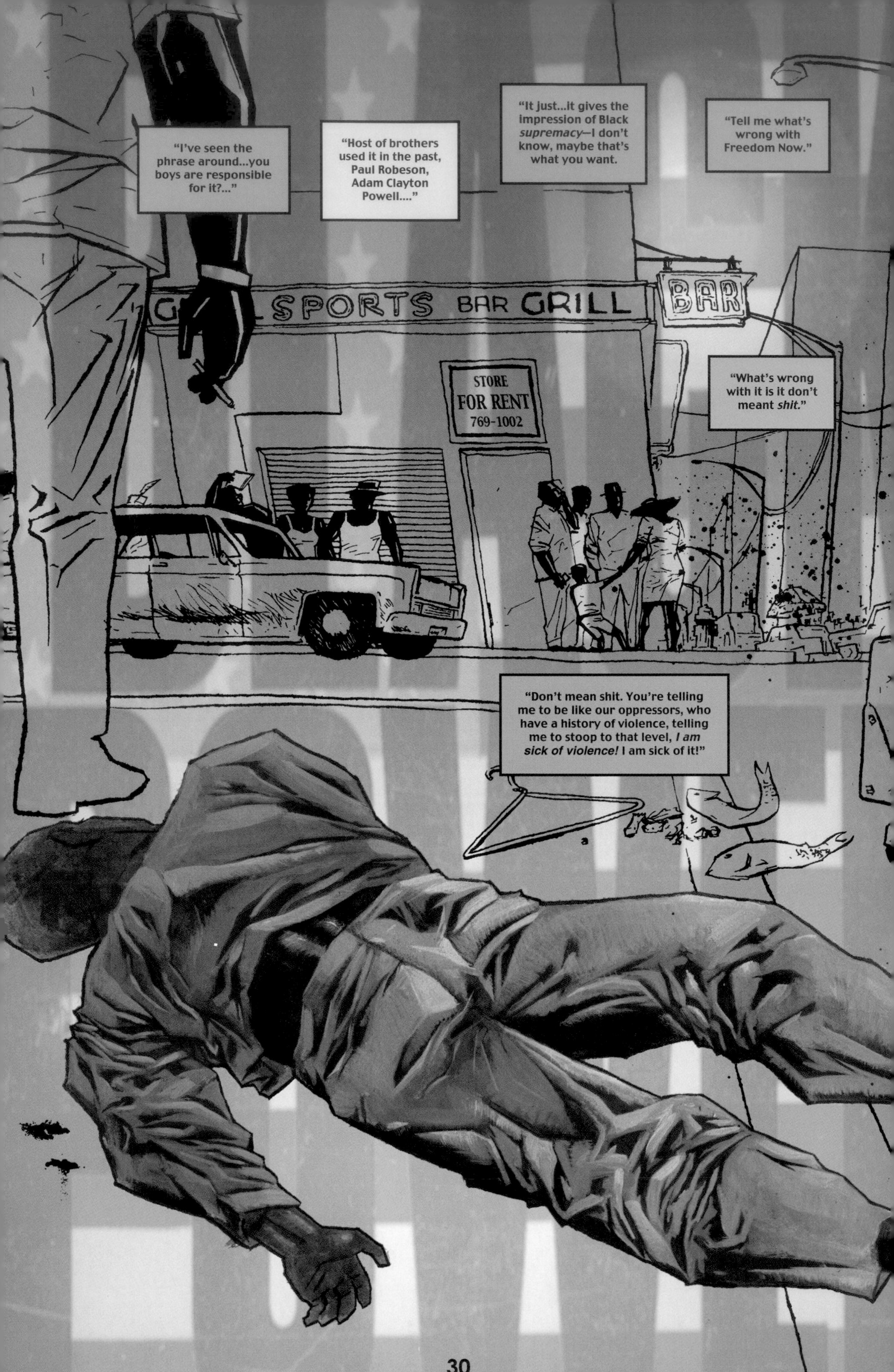
"I've seen the phrase around...you boys are responsible for it?..."
"Host of brothers used it in the past, Paul Robeson, Adam Clayton Powell...."
"It just...it gives the impression of Black *supremacy*—I don't know, maybe that's what you want.
"Tell me what's wrong with Freedom Now."
SPORTS BAR GRILL
BAR
STORE FOR RENT 769-1002
"What's wrong with it is it don't meant *shit*."
"Don't mean shit. You're telling me to be like our oppressors, who have a history of violence, telling me to stoop to that level, *I am sick of violence!* I am sick of it!"

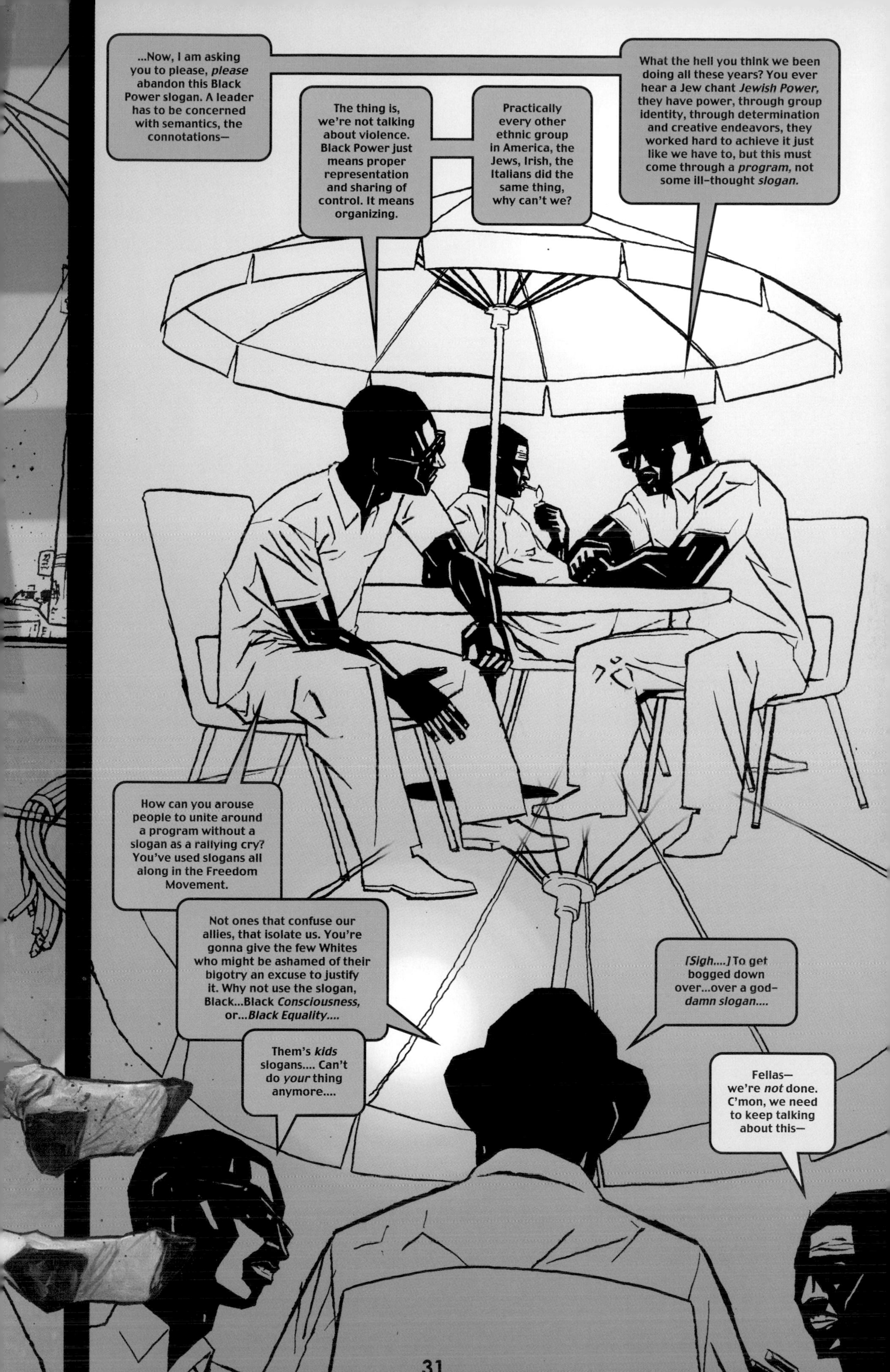

...Now, I am asking you to please, *please* abandon this Black Power slogan. A leader has to be concerned with semantics, the connotations—
The thing is, we're not talking about violence. Black Power just means proper representation and sharing of control. It means organizing.
Practically every other ethnic group in America, the Jews, Irish, the Italians did the same thing, why can't we?
What the hell you think we been doing all these years? You ever hear a Jew chant *Jewish Power,* they have power, through group identity, through determination and creative endeavors, they worked hard to achieve it just like we have to, but this must come through a *program,* not some ill-thought *slogan.*
How can you arouse people to unite around a program without a slogan as a rallying cry? You've used slogans all along in the Freedom Movement.
Not ones that confuse our allies, that isolate us. You're gonna give the few Whites who might be ashamed of their bigotry an excuse to justify it. Why not use the slogan, Black...Black *Consciousness,* or...*Black Equality....*
Them's *kids* slogans.... Can't do *your* thing anymore....
[Sigh....] To get bogged down over...over a god-*damn slogan....*
Fellas— we're *not* done. C'mon, we need to keep talking about this—

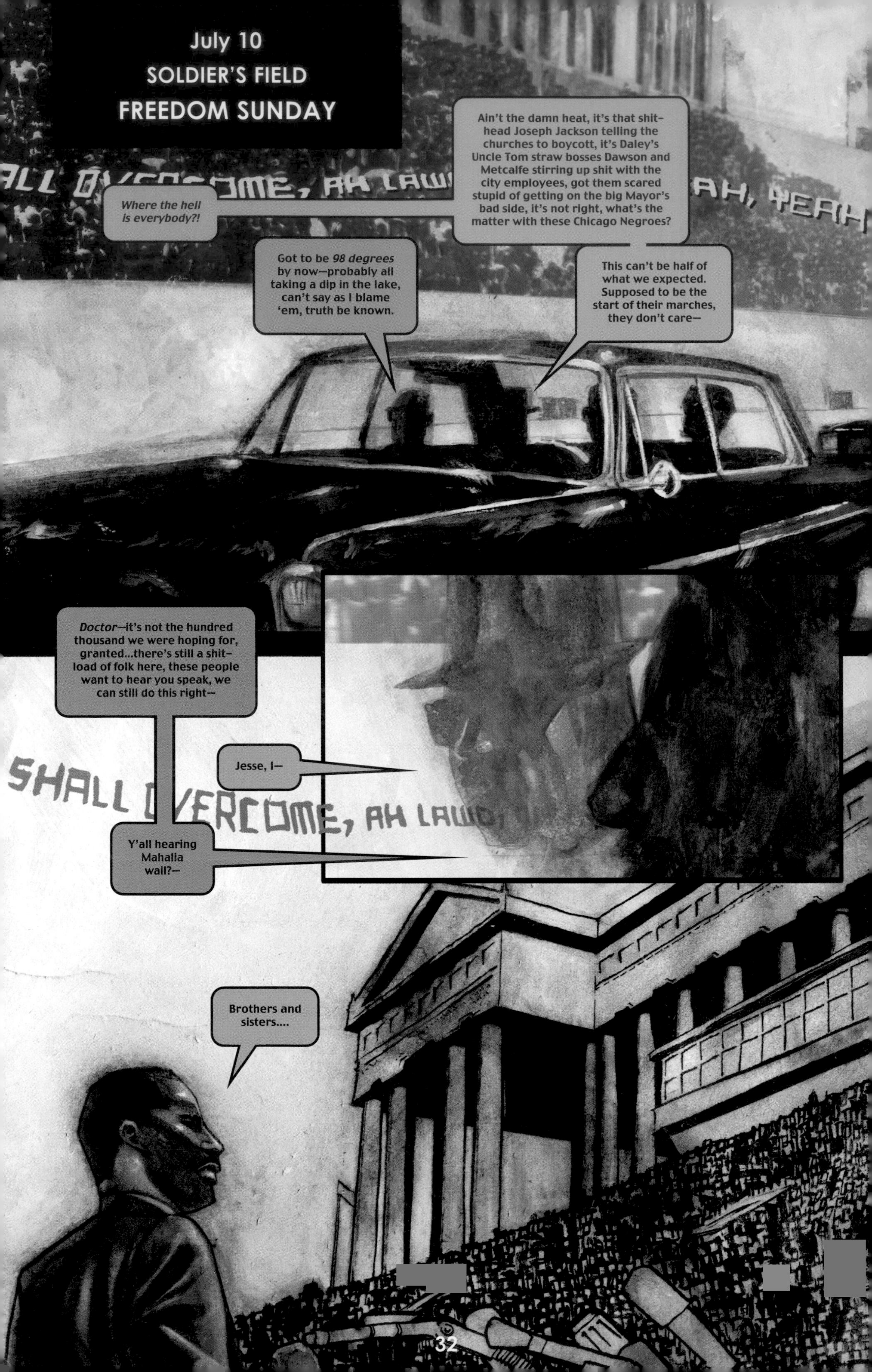

July 10
SOLDIER'S FIELD
FREEDOM SUNDAY
Where the hell is everybody?!
Ain't the damn heat, it's that shit-head Joseph Jackson telling the churches to boycott, it's Daley's Uncle Tom straw bosses Dawson and Metcalfe stirring up shit with the city employees, got them scared stupid of getting on the big Mayor's bad side, it's not right, what's the matter with these Chicago Negroes?
Got to be *98 degrees* by now—probably all taking a dip in the lake, can't say as I blame 'em, truth be known.
This can't be half of what we expected. Supposed to be the start of their marches, they don't care—
Doctor—it's not the hundred thousand we were hoping for, granted...there's still a shit-load of folk here, these people want to hear you speak, we can still do this right—
Jesse, I—
SHALL OVERCOME, AH LAWD,
Y'all hearing Mahalia wail?—
Brothers and sisters....

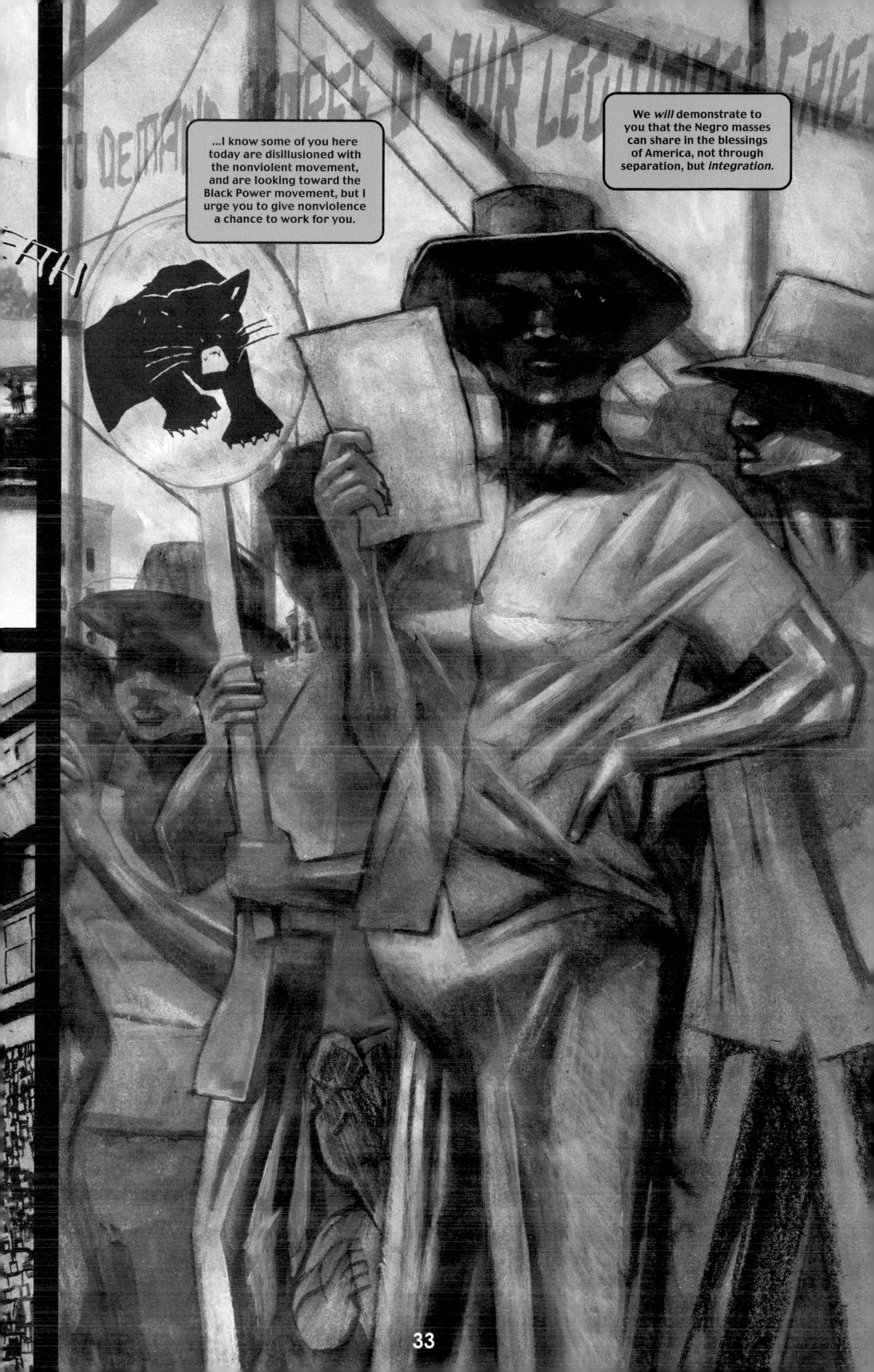
...I know some of you here today are disillusioned with the nonviolent movement, and are looking toward the Black Power movement, but I urge you to give nonviolence a chance to work for you.
We *will* demonstrate to you that the Negro masses can share in the blessings of America, not through separation, but *integration.*
TO DEMAND

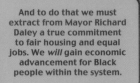

And to do that we must extract from Mayor Richard Daley a true commitment to fair housing and equal jobs. We *will* gain economic advancement for Black people within the system.

And to do *that* we need to organize ourselves and consolidate our economic and political resources.

Black people of Chicago, I call on you to withdraw your money from all banks and finance houses that discriminate against you, and to boycott any company that refuses to employ an adequate number of Negroes, Puerto Ricans, and other ethnic minorities in better paying jobs.

CIC FREE

CHICAGO CIC

34

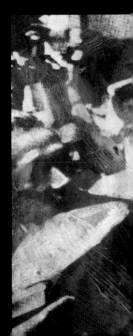

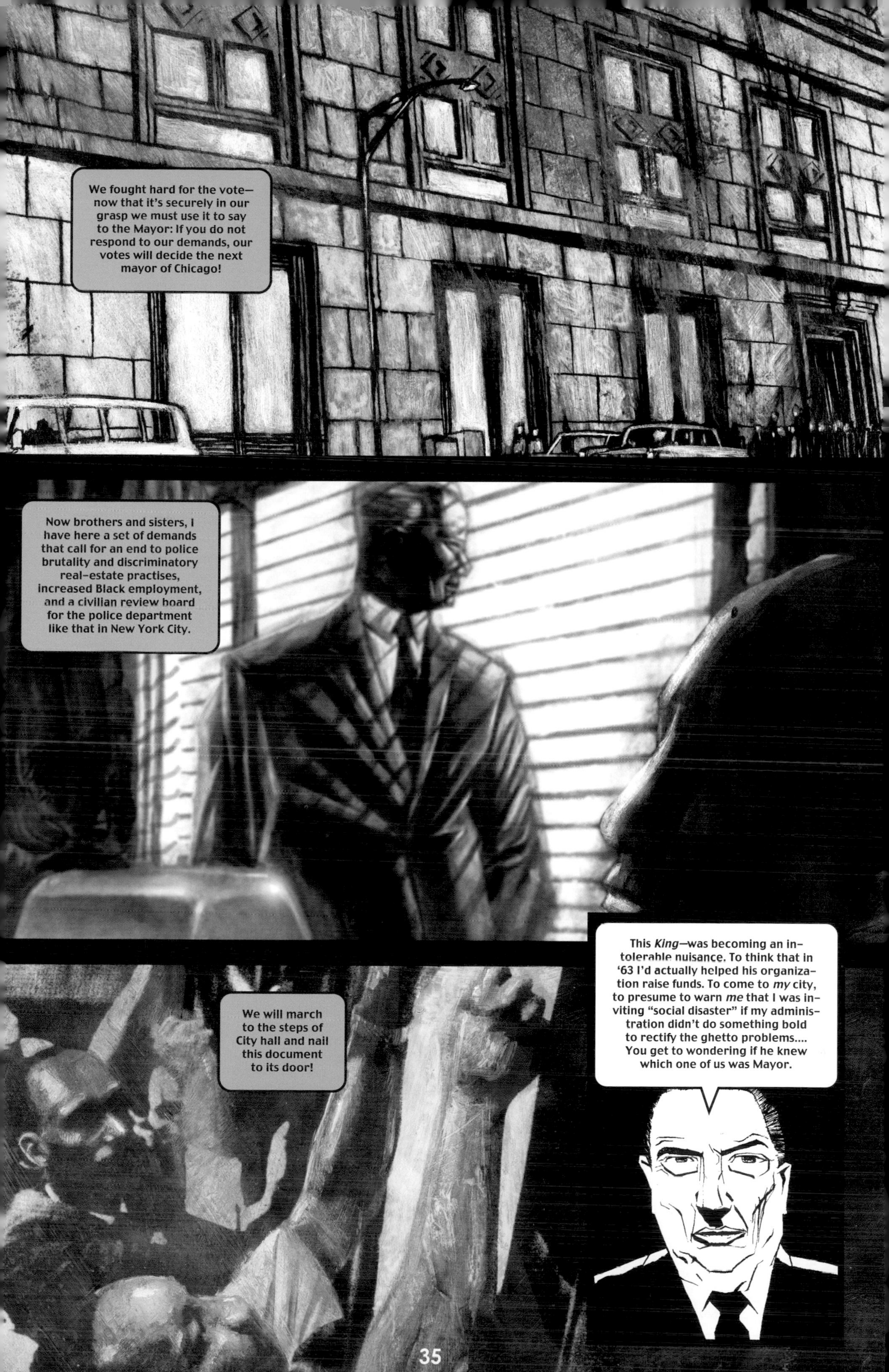
We fought hard for the vote—now that it's securely in our grasp we must use it to say to the Mayor: If you do not respond to our demands, our votes will decide the next mayor of Chicago!
Now brothers and sisters, I have here a set of demands that call for an end to police brutality and discriminatory real-estate practises, increased Black employment, and a civilian review board for the police department like that in New York City.
We will march to the steps of City hall and nail this document to its door!
This *King*—was becoming an intolerable nuisance. To think that in '63 I'd actually helped his organization raise funds. To come to *my* city, to presume to warn *me* that I was inviting "social disaster" if my administration didn't do something bold to rectify the ghetto problems.... You get to wondering if he knew which one of us was Mayor.

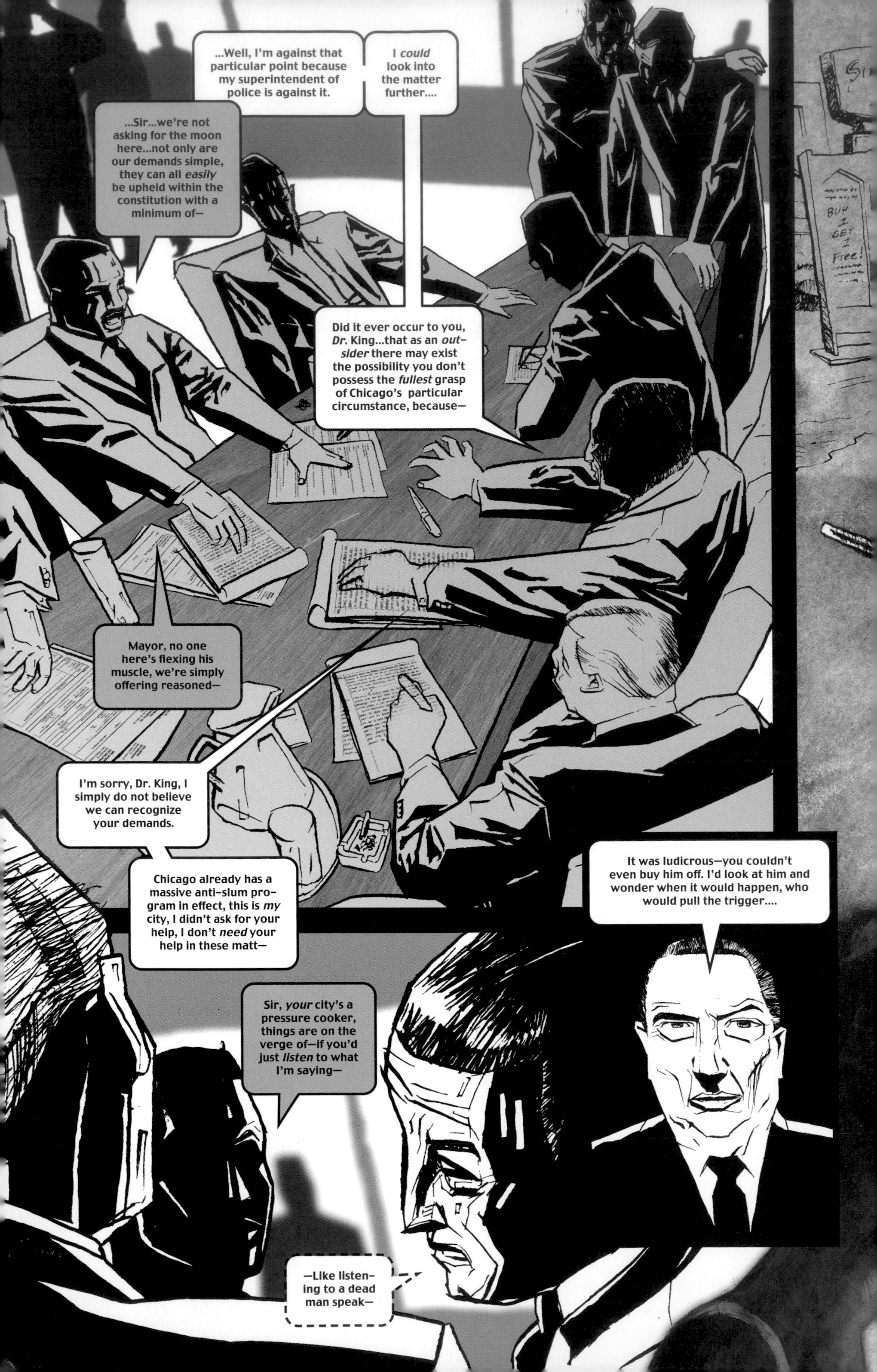

...Well, I'm against that particular point because my superintendent of police is against it.
I *could* look into the matter further....
...Sir...we're not asking for the moon here...not only are our demands simple, they can all *easily* be upheld within the constitution with a minimum of—
Did it ever occur to you, *Dr.* King...that as an *out-sider* there may exist the possibility you don't possess the *fullest* grasp of Chicago's particular circumstance, because—
Mayor, no one here's flexing his muscle, we're simply offering reasoned—
I'm sorry, Dr. King, I simply do not believe we can recognize your demands.
Chicago already has a massive anti-slum program in effect, this is *my* city, I didn't ask for your help, I don't *need* your help in these matt—
It was ludicrous—you couldn't even buy him off. I'd look at him and wonder when it would happen, who would pull the trigger....
Sir, *your* city's a pressure cooker, things are on the verge of—if you'd just *listen* to what I'm saying—
—Like listening to a dead man speak—
BUY 1 GET 1 Free!

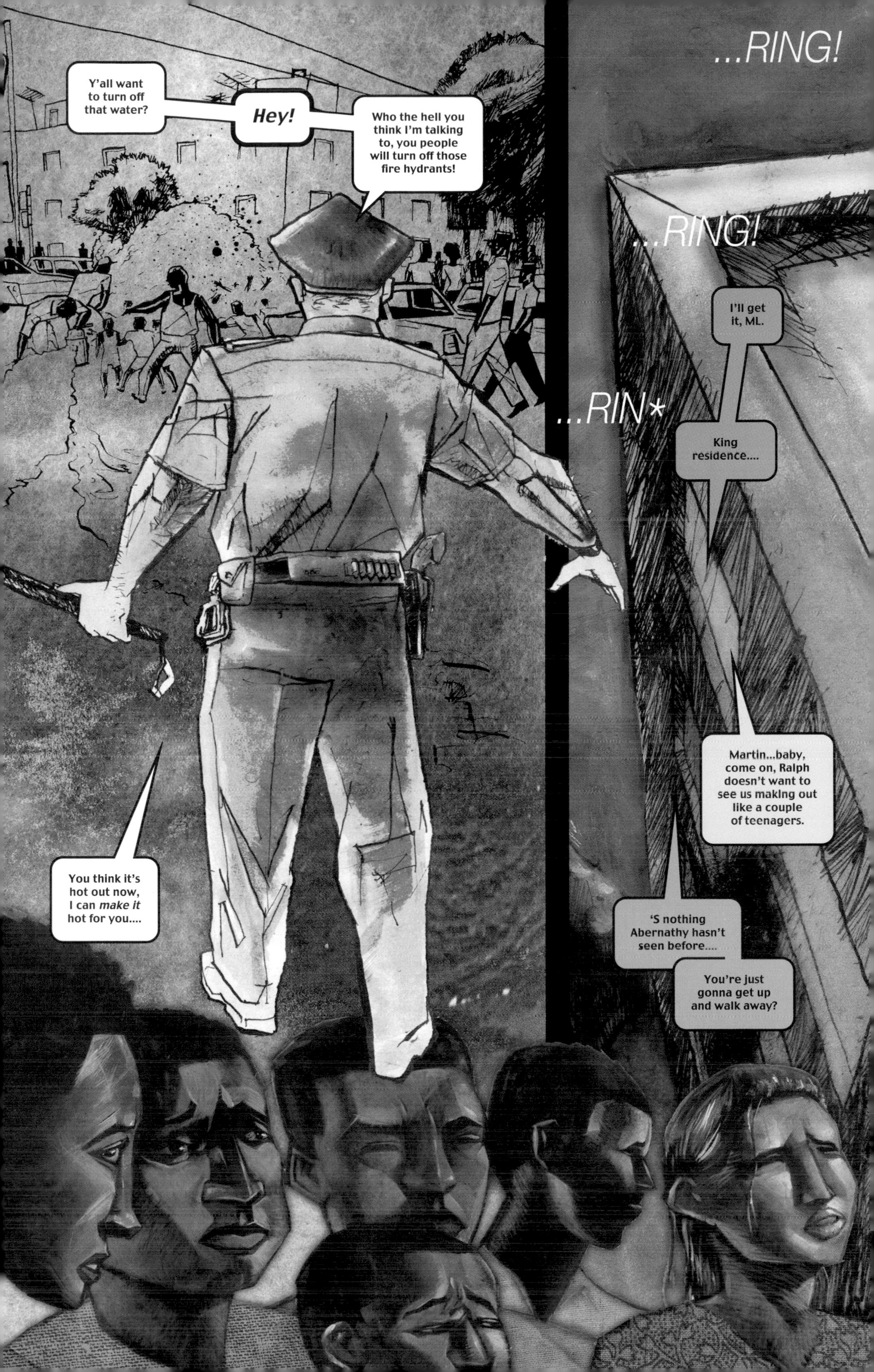
Y'all want to turn off that water?
Hey!
Who the hell you think I'm talking to, you people will turn off those fire hydrants!
You think it's hot out now, I can *make it* hot for you....
...RING!
...RING!
...RIN*
I'll get it, ML.
King residence....
Martin...baby, come on, Ralph doesn't want to see us making out like a couple of teenagers.
'S nothing Abernathy hasn't seen before....
You're just gonna get up and walk away?

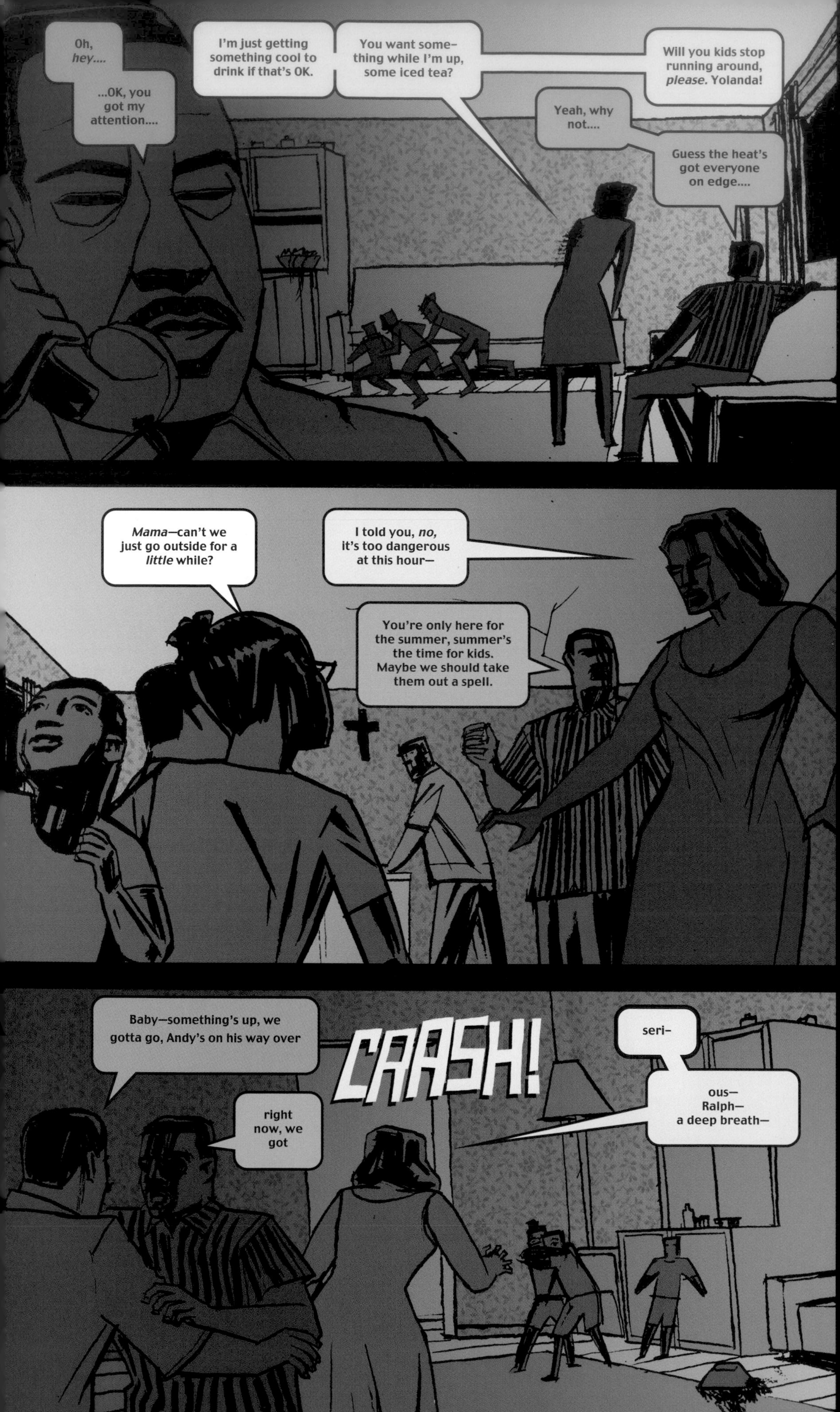
Oh, *hey*....
...OK, you got my attention....
I'm just getting something cool to drink if that's OK.
You want something while I'm up, some iced tea?
Will you kids stop running around, *please.* Yolanda!
Yeah, why not....
Guess the heat's got everyone on edge....
Mama—can't we just go outside for a *little* while?
I told you, *no,* it's too dangerous at this hour—
You're only here for the summer, summer's the time for kids. Maybe we should take them out a spell.
Baby—something's up, we gotta go, Andy's on his way over
right now, we got
CRASH!
seri-
ous— Ralph— a deep breath—

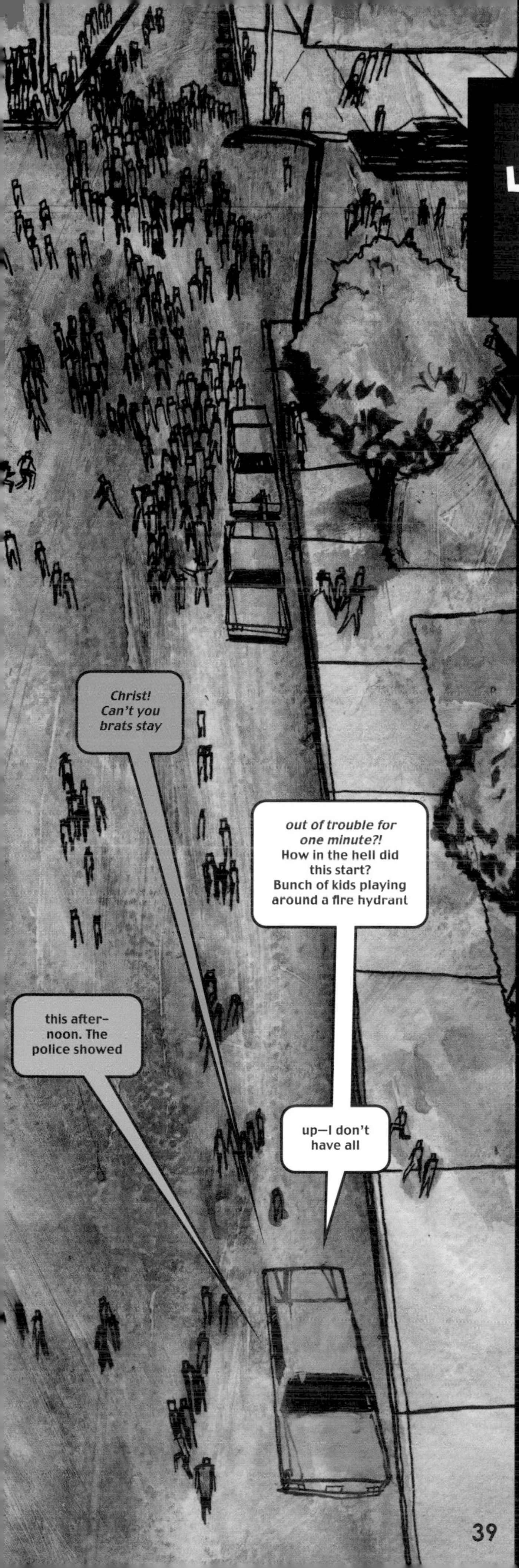
Christ! Can't you brats stay
out of trouble for one minute?! How in the hell did this start? Bunch of kids playing around a fire hydrant
this after-noon. The police showed
up—I don't have all

JULY 12

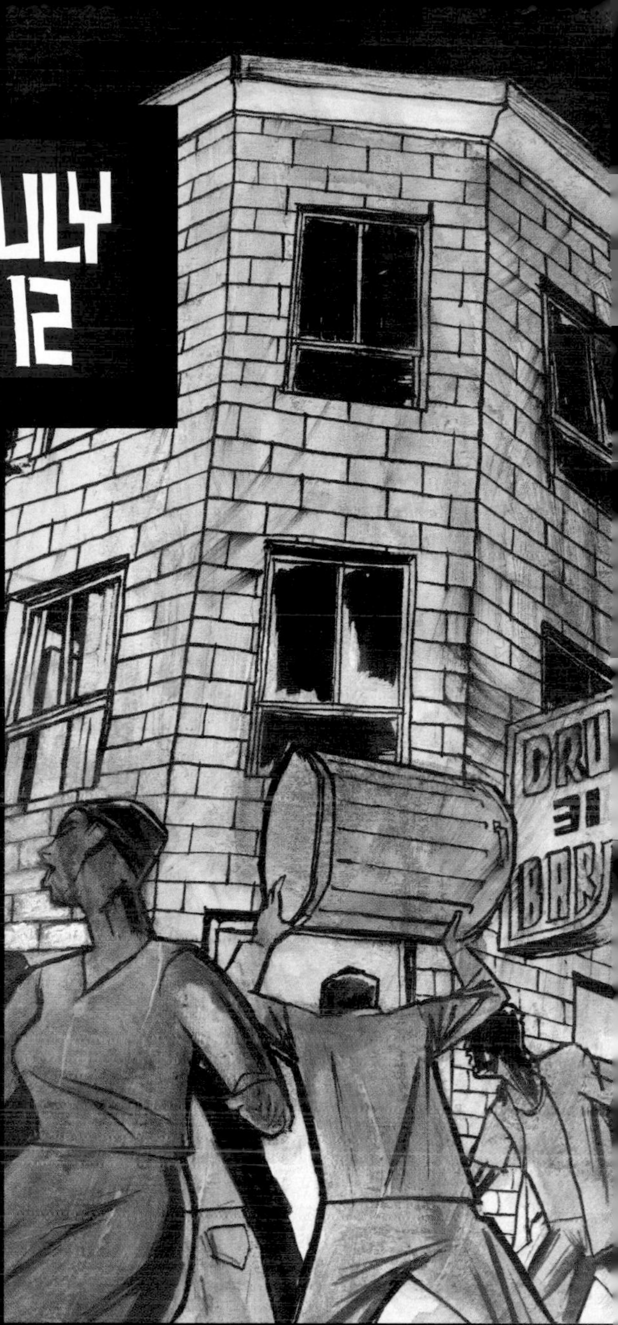
DRI
31
BAR

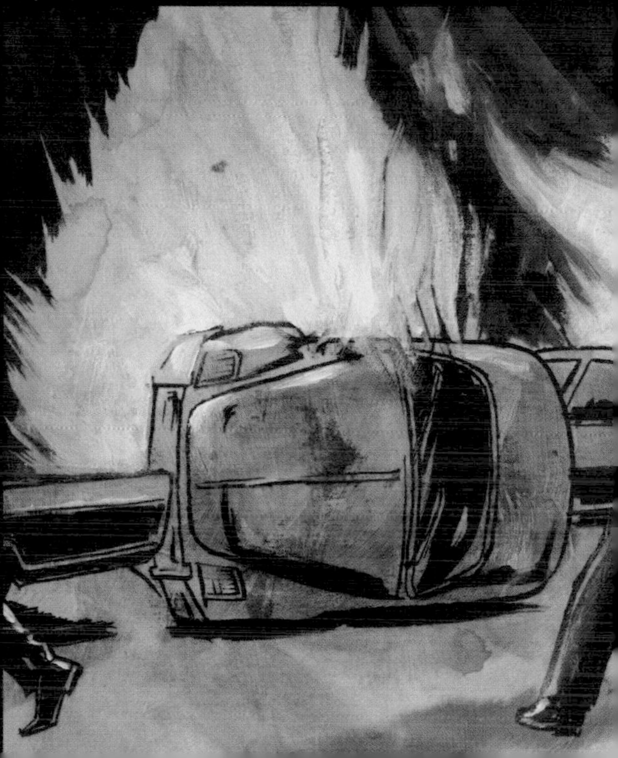

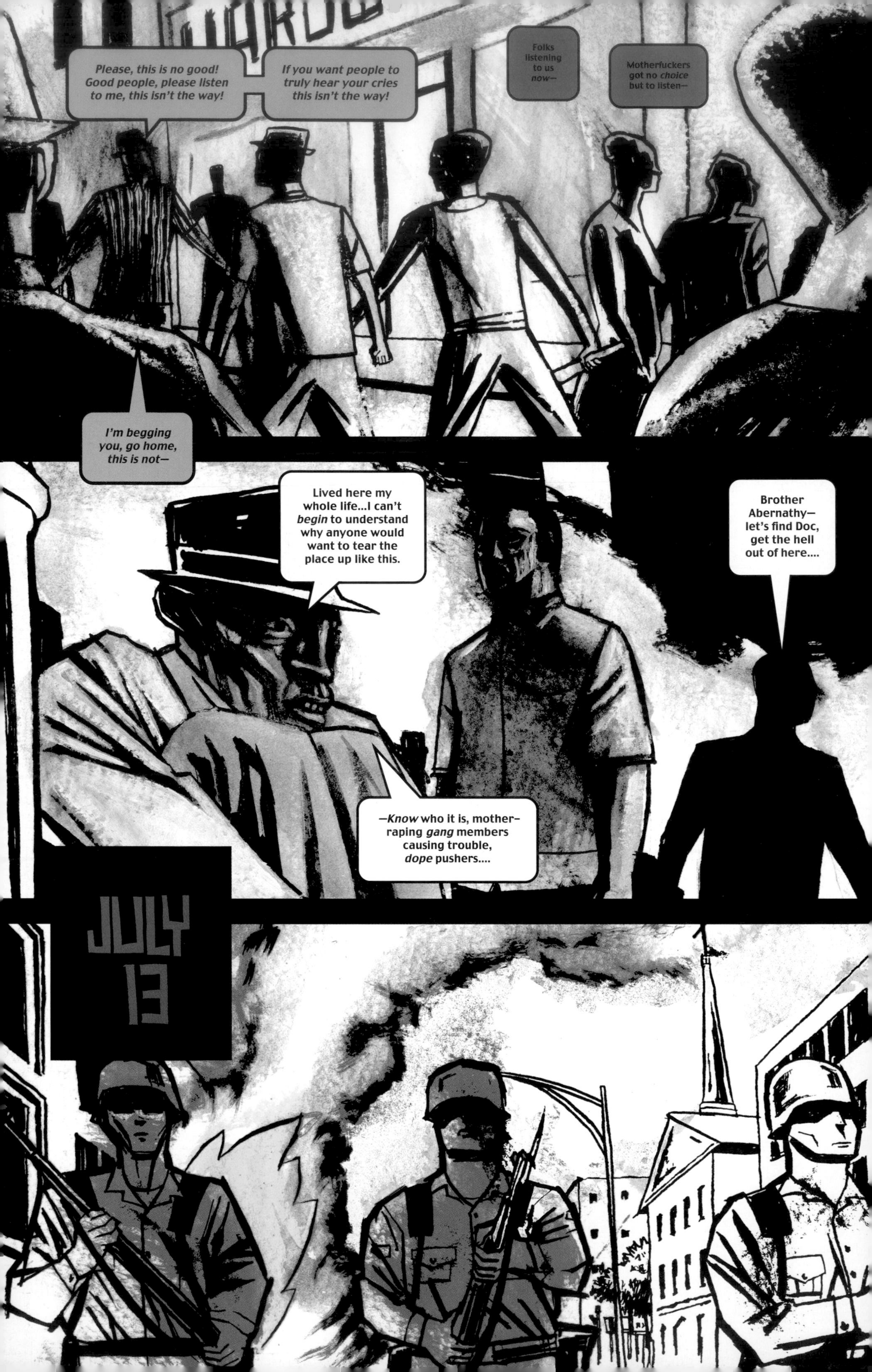
Please, this is no good! Good people, please listen to me, this isn't the way!
If you want people to truly hear your cries this isn't the way!
Folks listening to us now—
Motherfuckers got no choice but to listen—
I'm begging you, go home, this is not—
Lived here my whole life...I can't begin to understand why anyone would want to tear the place up like this.
—Know who it is, mother-raping gang members causing trouble, dope pushers....
Brother Abernathy—let's find Doc, get the hell out of here....
JULY 13

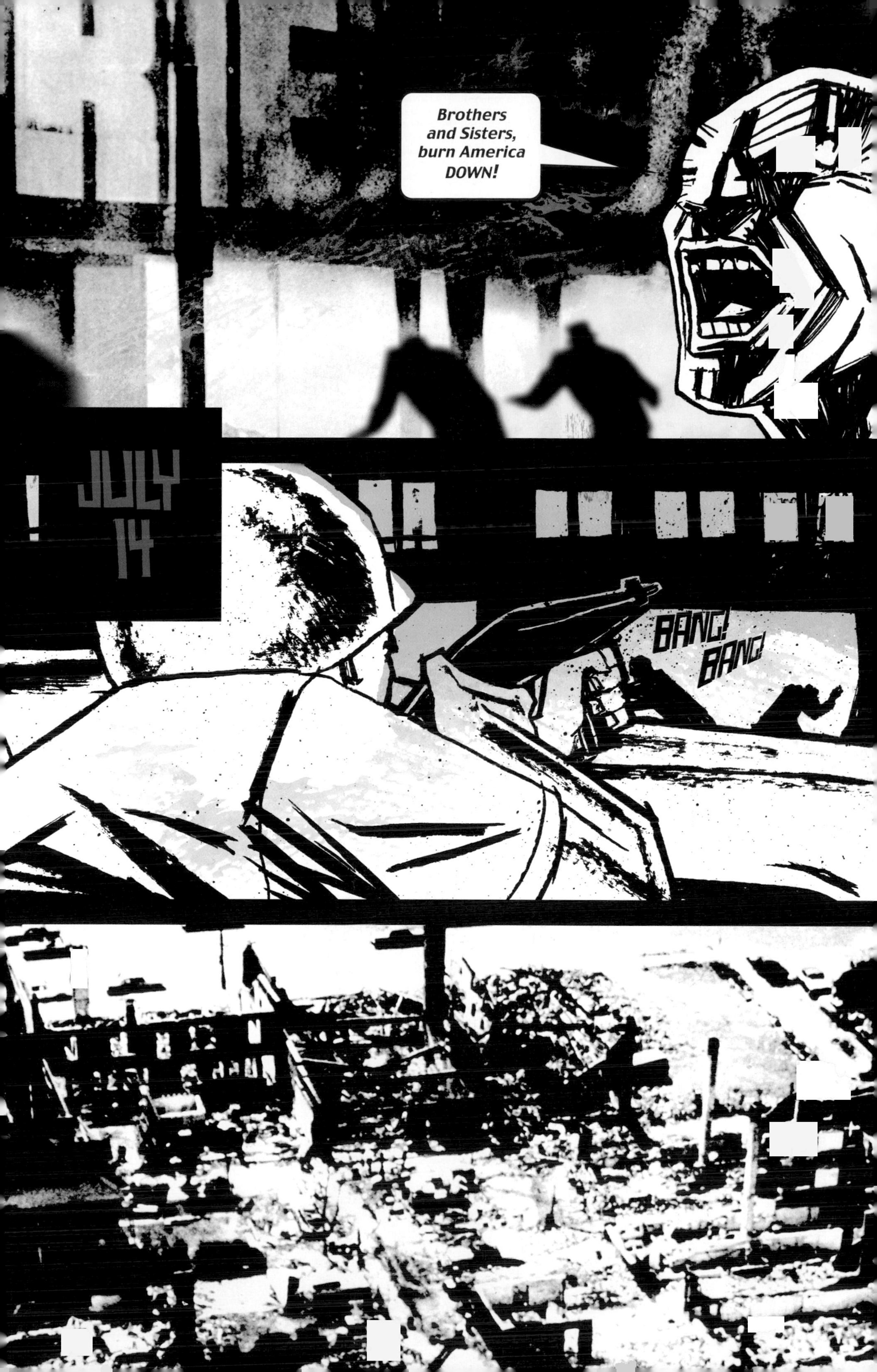
Brothers and Sisters, burn America DOWN!
JULY 14
BANG! BANG!

By and large gang members were responsible for the violence of those three nights, for actually instigating and perpetuating it, although the cops certainly provided their fair share.... I don't think it's an accident the violence followed a line to City Hall and that it was mostly White–owned stores that were bombed.

Two people were killed, I think 56 injured...272 thrown in jail, give or take.... Mayor Daley went off, he blamed the riots on anarchists, Communists, and Dr. King's own staff, something about instructing rioters on violence by showing them films on Watts.

All of a sudden Daley was eager to sit down with King and was persuaded to make *some* concessions, anything to ensure there was no more rioting. I don't remember anybody being too thrilled with what was done.

Moved in a few more swimming pools, some sprinklers on the fire hydrants, just so we could escape the heat a bit during those Chicago summers. Someone set up a citizens committee to study the police department.... But you have to ask what these so-called *concessions* really changed.... Nine months in a place, at the end you're still an outsider...I don't think the SCLC really knew what to ask for....

I believe it was probably around this time some of the youth gangs began to see that perhaps civil disobedience was slightly more effective a strategy than aimless rioting, which as a White person I couldn't agree with more, *ha, ha, ha*....

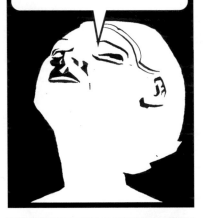

...So...some agreed to join King in the Chicago marches, that was good. ...I should point out that the initial marches proved to be among the most violent—well, certainly of anything *I've* seen, and from what I understand, certainly of *King's* career. Thousands of screaming people surrounding a couple of hundred marchers. And not just the men, you had housewives throwing rocks, you had *children*....

In retrospect I realize it was probably just plain *tough* for us Chicagoans to face up to the hate King exposed here. Newspaper editors, politicians...so many voices vilifying King, accusing *him* of creating the city's racial tensions, insisting he stop the marches. I remember thinking even at that time that his life was probably in danger.

You want us to stop marching, then make justice a reality. I don't mind saying to Chicago I'm tired of marching for something that should've been mine at birth, I'm tired of living every day under the threat of death. I have no martyr complex, I want to live as long as anybody.

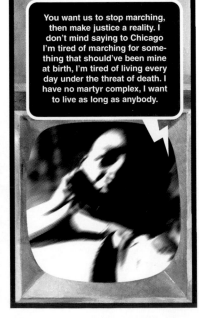

A new march was announced in Cicero, which is a suburb outside Cook County. Now, you have to understand about *Cicero*...if you were Black, you just didn't cross the viaduct into Cicero, driving through, you just didn't get a flat, 'cause as a nigger, they see you getting out to change your tire....

One Black kid got murdered there while looking for work. A Black family tried to move in there, had to be fifty-one, fifty-two—the shit got so bad with Whites rioting and stuff the National Guard had to be called in, serious. *One* family and this happens.

So King tells the world he's gonna march there, he's gonna show everybody how rough Chicago is and force the Mayor to fix the slums, and suddenly he's got even the Black Power guys on his side. It was something. I mean, this was a very radical fucking move. Could've embarrassed a lot of politicians.

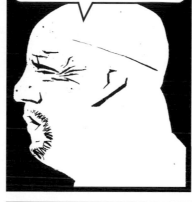

So it comes down to a show-down between Daley and King, championship fight, going for the belt, got their poker faces on, and Daley, *pussy* that he was, backs down, hey, thank *God*. He agrees to sit down again with King which was the same as admitting there actually was something wrong with Chicago's housing policies, something he'd always denied.

They came up with something called the *Summit Agreement.* Without getting lost in detail, this agreement was...it was *OK*, it was a good start. It helped get some families into nice homes, shit like that. But surprise, surprise, it didn't go far enough.

King had Daley on the ropes, he should've kept slugging him, not just get a few families out the ghetto, 'cause what about the rest of us left here? I mean, some of them Black Power motherfuckers even threatened to march on Cicero anyway.

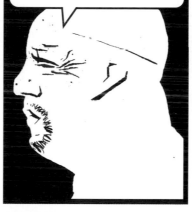

Daley stood with King in front of the cameras saying, "This is a great day for Chicago," promised to uphold his end of the agreement, turned around and did exactly jack shit. Shaking hands like they were drinking buddies or something. He was a crafty bastard, devious, an old hand at manipulating people, saying the right things to get what he wanted.

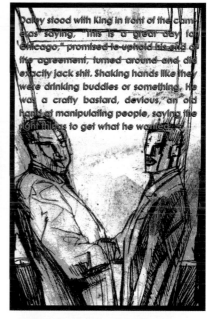

That Summit Agreement was a sell-out. Just a way for that King to bail out of Chi-town and not look like an asshole. And don't let nobody tell you it was 'cause'a Carl Stokes Mayoral campaign neither. You see how fast they got out of Chicago after making the agreement, tell me I'm wrong....

...If the guy had just continued to *push* Daley...but like always he backed off just when he should have fought harder. Fuck that nonviolence shit—even today, what we need to get is some of that *Black Power*....

Let's face it. Most... maybe all the people here are going to remain here until the day they meet their maker. Morally, when we *say* Freedom Now, we should *have* freedom now, we should *expect* freedom now...the fact is it doesn't all *come* now....

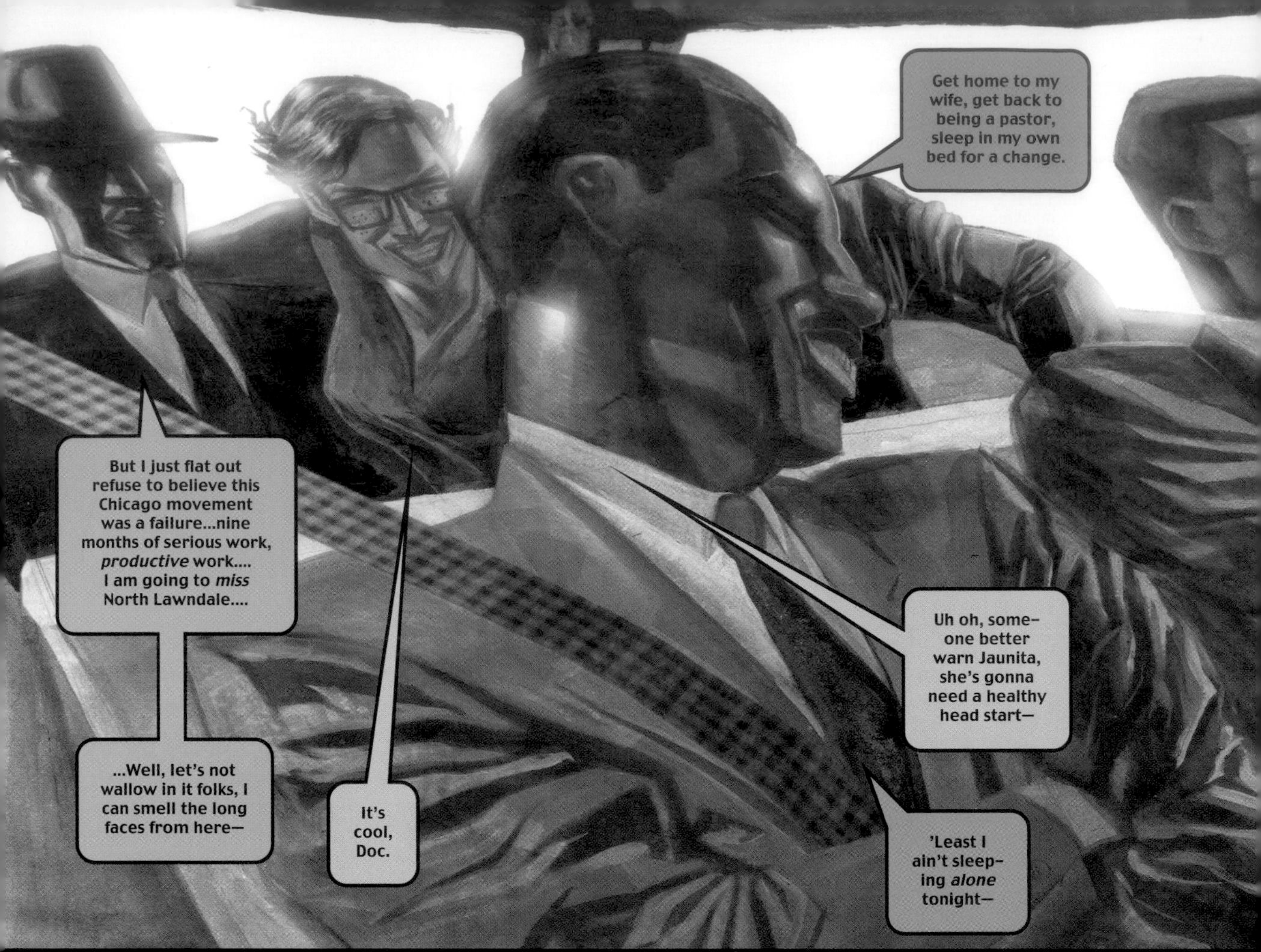
Get home to my wife, get back to being a pastor, sleep in my own bed for a change.
But I just flat out refuse to believe this Chicago movement was a failure...nine months of serious work, *productive* work.... I am going to *miss* North Lawndale....
Uh oh, someone better warn Jaunita, she's gonna need a healthy head start—
...Well, let's not wallow in it folks, I can smell the long faces from here—
It's cool, Doc.
'Least I ain't sleeping *alone* tonight—

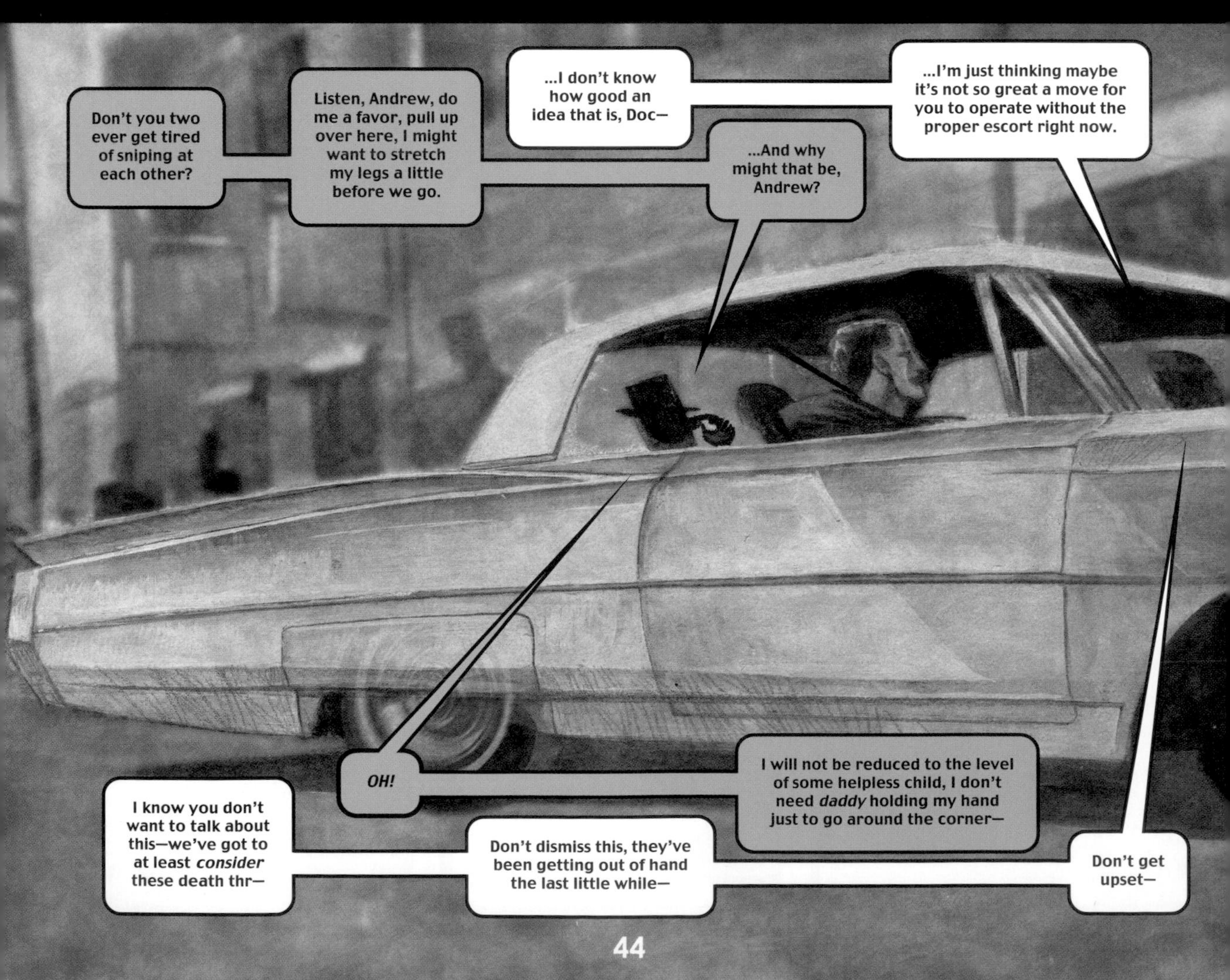
Don't you two ever get tired of sniping at each other?
Listen, Andrew, do me a favor, pull up over here, I might want to stretch my legs a little before we go.
...I don't know how good an idea that is, Doc—
...I'm just thinking maybe it's not so great a move for you to operate without the proper escort right now.
...And why might that be, Andrew?
OH!
I will not be reduced to the level of some helpless child, I don't need *daddy* holding my hand just to go around the corner—
I know you don't want to talk about this—we've got to at least *consider* these death thr—
Don't dismiss this, they've been getting out of hand the last little while—
Don't get upset—

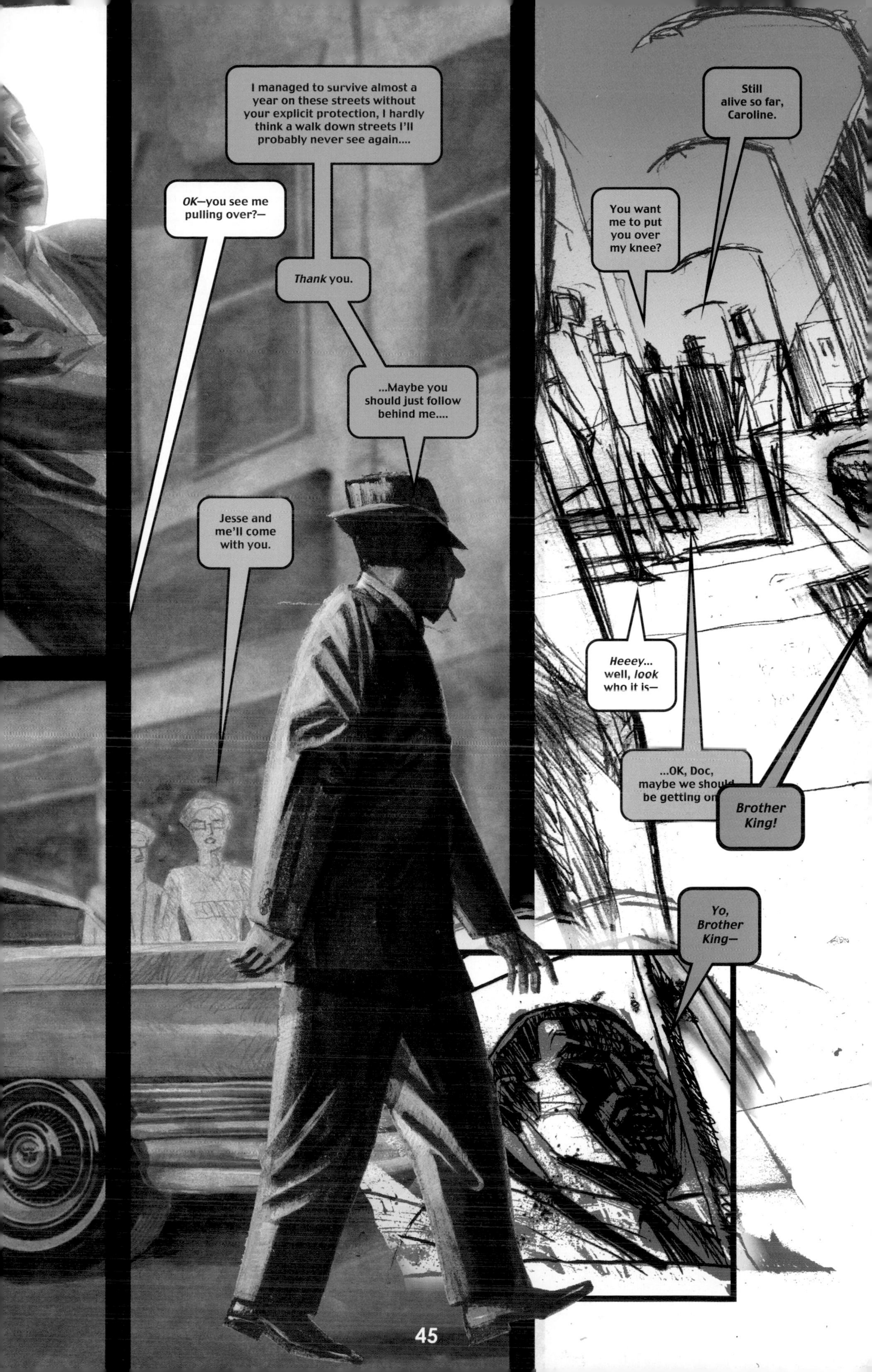

OK—you see me pulling over?—
I managed to survive almost a year on these streets without your explicit protection, I hardly think a walk down streets I'll probably never see again....
Thank you.
...Maybe you should just follow behind me....
Jesse and me'll come with you.
Still alive so far, Caroline.
You want me to put you over my knee?
Heeey... well, look who it is—
...OK, Doc, maybe we shoul be getting on
Brother King!
Yo, Brother King—

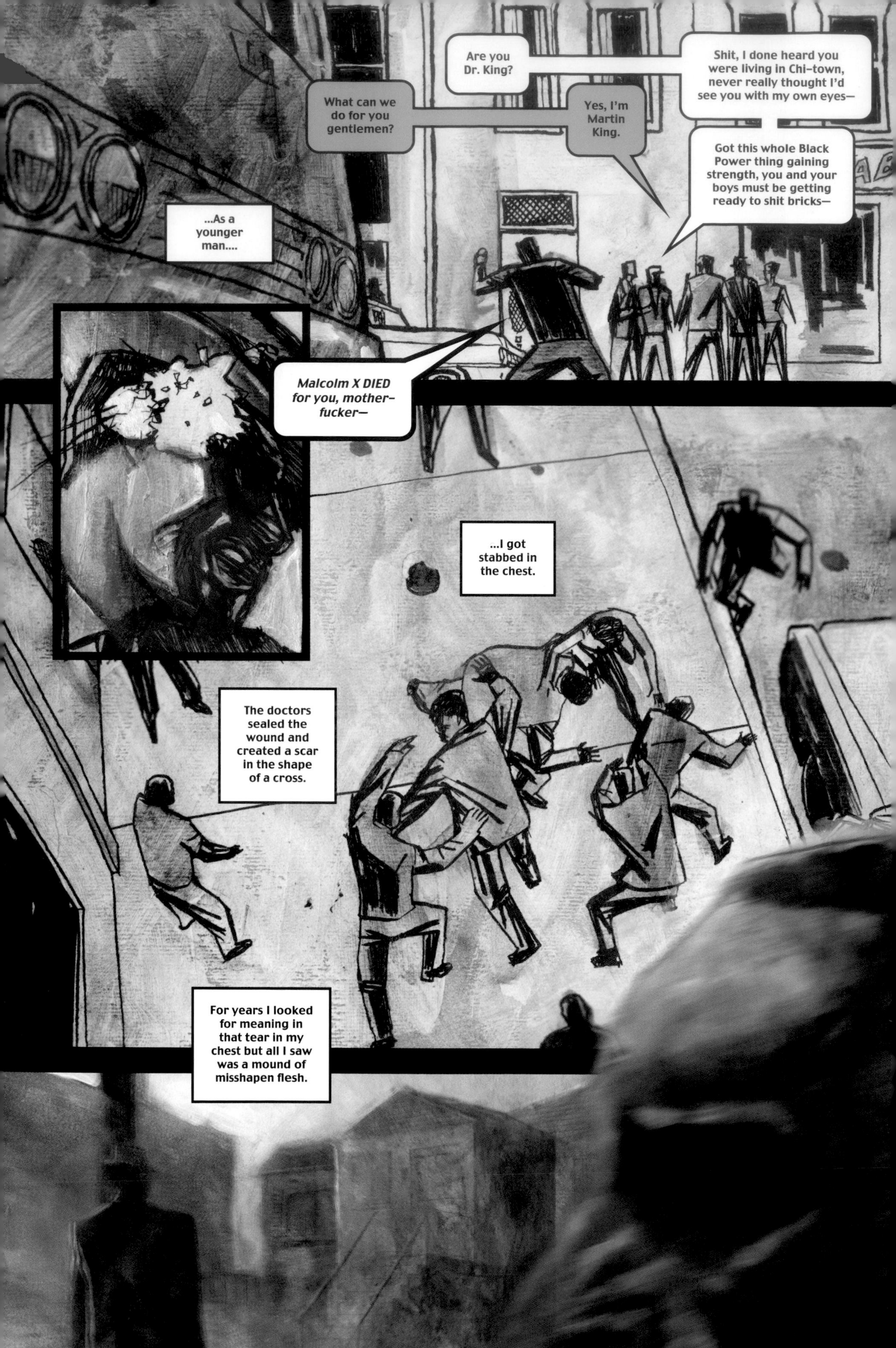
...As a younger man....
Are you Dr. King?
What can we do for you gentlemen?
Yes, I'm Martin King.
Shit, I done heard you were living in Chi-town, never really thought I'd see you with my own eyes—
Got this whole Black Power thing gaining strength, you and your boys must be getting ready to shit bricks—
Malcolm X DIED for you, mother-fucker—
...I got stabbed in the chest.
The doctors sealed the wound and created a scar in the shape of a cross.
For years I looked for meaning in that tear in my chest but all I saw was a mound of misshapen flesh.

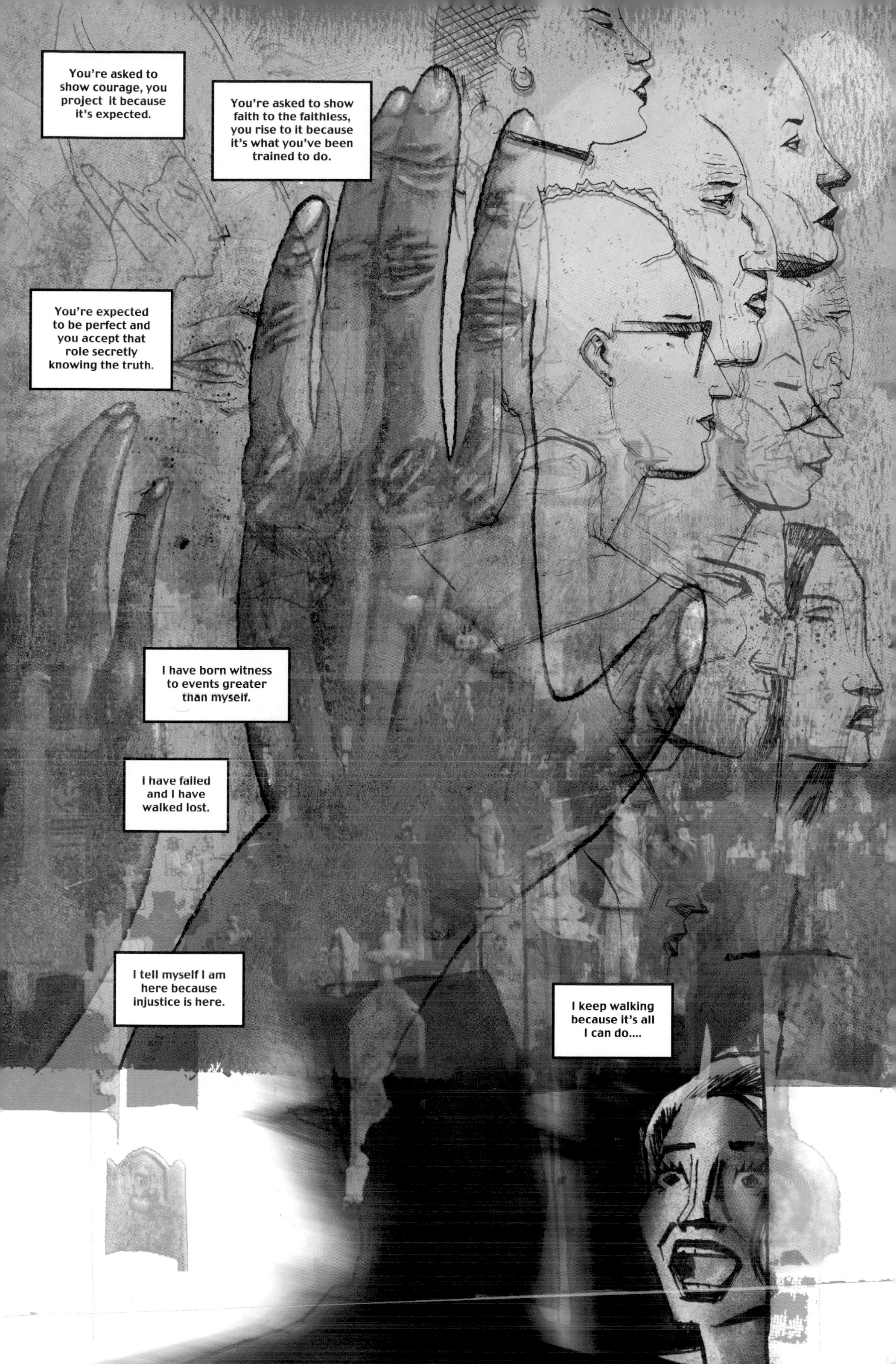
You're asked to show courage, you project it because it's expected.
You're asked to show faith to the faithless, you rise to it because it's what you've been trained to do.
You're expected to be perfect and you accept that role secretly knowing the truth.
I have born witness to events greater than myself.
I have failed and I have walked lost.
I tell myself I am here because injustice is here.
I keep walking because it's all I can do....

I have here part of the transcription of a meeting between Black Power advocates and Martin...just a suggestion of some of the feelings of the time. In the fall of sixty-six, Stokely Carmichael was crossing the country speaking out against Vietnam...

—And denouncing integration, basically championing our awakening Black masses' so-called "*revolutionary*" ideology," if you will, which to my way of thinking is a catch phrase covering most of what Black Power meant.

The sentiment was that violence was psychologically healthy and tactically sound, that only violence could bring about Black liberation. The feeling was that nonviolence, that "progress" belonged to *middle-class* Blacks and Whites. So, reading Martin's reply, it says here,

The courageous efforts of our own insurrectionist brothers, such as Denmark Vesey and Nat Turner should be eloquent reminders that violent rebellion is doomed from the start. Negroes in this country are outnumbered ten to one,

so what are the chances and potential casualties of a minority rebellion against a rich and heavily armed majority with a fanatical right wing that would delight in exterminating thousands of Black people? Violence only multiplies hate, intensifying the brutality

"—of the oppressor and the bitterness of the oppressed. Only *love* can drive out *hate*." Had to be rough. After the failure of the Chicago movement...and I see no need to be charitable, let's confront the issue head on, it *was* a failure—Martin's credibility was sorely challenged.

The torch seemed to be passing to a new generation of leaders. More and more people were extolling the virtues of violence, "by any means necessary." Martin was accused of being out of step with the time, an anachronism of sorts.

In those appalling popularity polls his esteem was being challenged, even among prominent leaders; Adam Clayton Powell comes to mind, he publicly derided him, called him Martin Loser King. Very depressing, *galling* time for him....

On April 4 of 1967, King delivered an address at my church, *Riverside* Church in New York, that put down *hard* America's growing involvement in Vietnam, 'cause by now there were 350,000 troops overseas. He said that America was spending too much time, money—

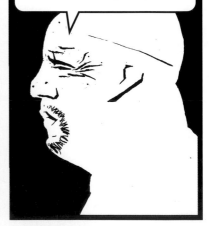

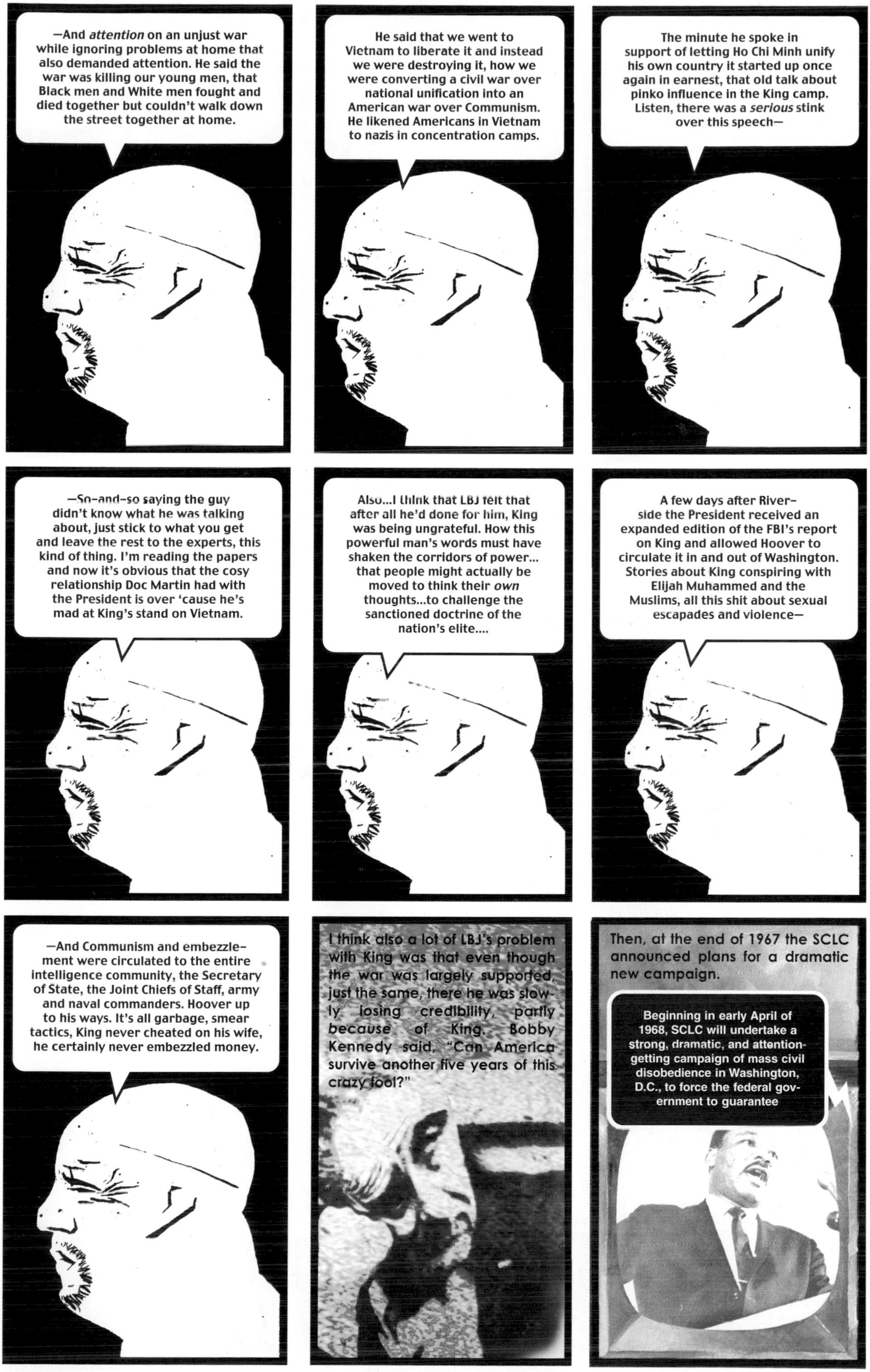
—And *attention* on an unjust war while ignoring problems at home that also demanded attention. He said the war was killing our young men, that Black men and White men fought and died together but couldn't walk down the street together at home.
He said that we went to Vietnam to liberate it and instead we were destroying it, how we were converting a civil war over national unification into an American war over Communism. He likened Americans in Vietnam to nazis in concentration camps.
The minute he spoke in support of letting Ho Chi Minh unify his own country it started up once again in earnest, that old talk about pinko influence in the King camp. Listen, there was a *serious* stink over this speech—
—So-and-so saying the guy didn't know what he was talking about, just stick to what you get and leave the rest to the experts, this kind of thing. I'm reading the papers and now it's obvious that the cosy relationship Doc Martin had with the President is over 'cause he's mad at King's stand on Vietnam.
Also...I think that LBJ felt that after all he'd done for him, King was being ungrateful. How this powerful man's words must have shaken the corridors of power... that people might actually be moved to think their *own* thoughts...to challenge the sanctioned doctrine of the nation's elite....
A few days after Riverside the President received an expanded edition of the FBI's report on King and allowed Hoover to circulate it in and out of Washington. Stories about King conspiring with Elijah Muhammed and the Muslims, all this shit about sexual escapades and violence—
—And Communism and embezzlement were circulated to the entire intelligence community, the Secretary of State, the Joint Chiefs of Staff, army and naval commanders. Hoover up to his ways. It's all garbage, smear tactics, King never cheated on his wife, he certainly never embezzled money.
I think also a lot of LBJ's problem with King was that even though the war was largely supported, just the same, there he was slowly losing credibility, partly *because* of King. Bobby Kennedy said, "Can America survive another five years of this crazy fool?"
Then, at the end of 1967 the SCLC announced plans for a dramatic new campaign.
Beginning in early April of 1968, SCLC will undertake a strong, dramatic, and attention-getting campaign of mass civil disobedience in Washington, D.C., to force the federal government to guarantee

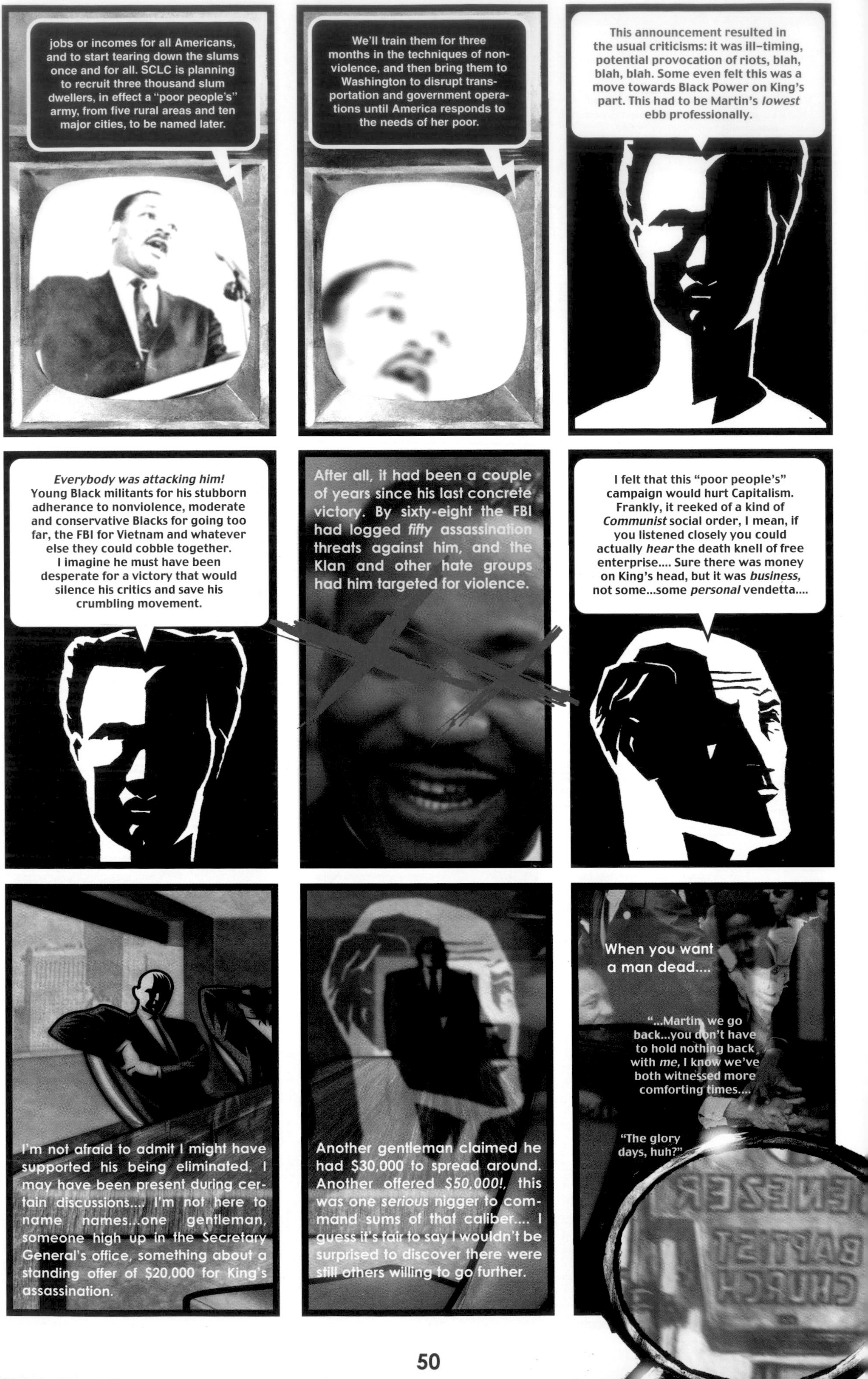
jobs or incomes for all Americans, and to start tearing down the slums once and for all. SCLC is planning to recruit three thousand slum dwellers, in effect a "poor people's" army, from five rural areas and ten major cities, to be named later.
We'll train them for three months in the techniques of non-violence, and then bring them to Washington to disrupt transportation and government operations until America responds to the needs of her poor.
This announcement resulted in the usual criticisms: it was ill-timing, potential provocation of riots, blah, blah, blah. Some even felt this was a move towards Black Power on King's part. This had to be Martin's *lowest* ebb professionally.
Everybody was attacking him! Young Black militants for his stubborn adherance to nonviolence, moderate and conservative Blacks for going too far, the FBI for Vietnam and whatever else they could cobble together. I imagine he must have been desperate for a victory that would silence his critics and save his crumbling movement.
After all, it had been a couple of years since his last concrete victory. By sixty-eight the FBI had logged *fifty* assassination threats against him, and the Klan and other hate groups had him targeted for violence.
I felt that this "poor people's" campaign would hurt Capitalism. Frankly, it reeked of a kind of *Communist* social order, I mean, if you listened closely you could actually *hear* the death knell of free enterprise.... Sure there was money on King's head, but it was *business*, not some...some *personal* vendetta....
I'm not afraid to admit I might have supported his being eliminated. I may have been present during certain discussions.... I'm not here to name names...one gentleman, someone high up in the Secretary General's office, something about a standing offer of $20,000 for King's assassination.
Another gentleman claimed he had $30,000 to spread around. Another offered *$50,000!*, this was one *serious* nigger to command sums of that caliber.... I guess it's fair to say I wouldn't be surprised to discover there were still others willing to go further.
When you want a man dead....
"...Martin, we go back...you don't have to hold nothing back with *me*, I know we've both witnessed more comforting times....
"The glory days, huh?"
ENEZER
BAPTIST
CHURCH

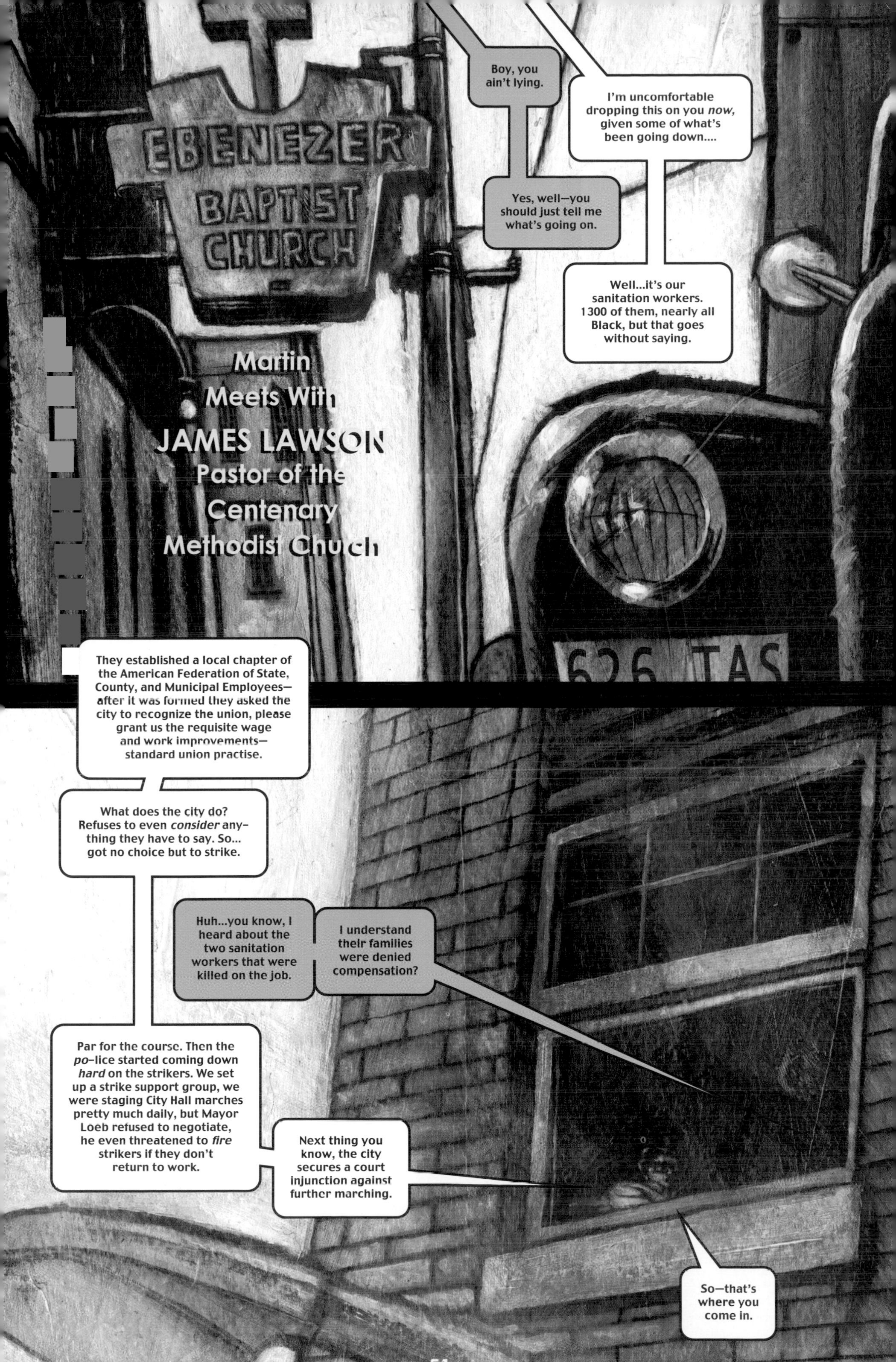
EBENEZER
BAPTIST
CHURCH
Boy, you ain't lying.
I'm uncomfortable dropping this on you *now*, given some of what's been going down....
Yes, well—you should just tell me what's going on.
Well...it's our sanitation workers. 1300 of them, nearly all Black, but that goes without saying.
Martin Meets With JAMES LAWSON Pastor of the Centenary Methodist Church
626 TAS
They established a local chapter of the American Federation of State, County, and Municipal Employees—after it was formed they asked the city to recognize the union, please grant us the requisite wage and work improvements—standard union practise.
What does the city do? Refuses to even *consider* anything they have to say. So... got no choice but to strike.
Huh...you know, I heard about the two sanitation workers that were killed on the job.
I understand their families were denied compensation?
Par for the course. Then the *po*–lice started coming down *hard* on the strikers. We set up a strike support group, we were staging City Hall marches pretty much daily, but Mayor Loeb refused to negotiate, he even threatened to *fire* strikers if they don't return to work.
Next thing you know, the city secures a court injunction against further marching.
So—that's where you come in.

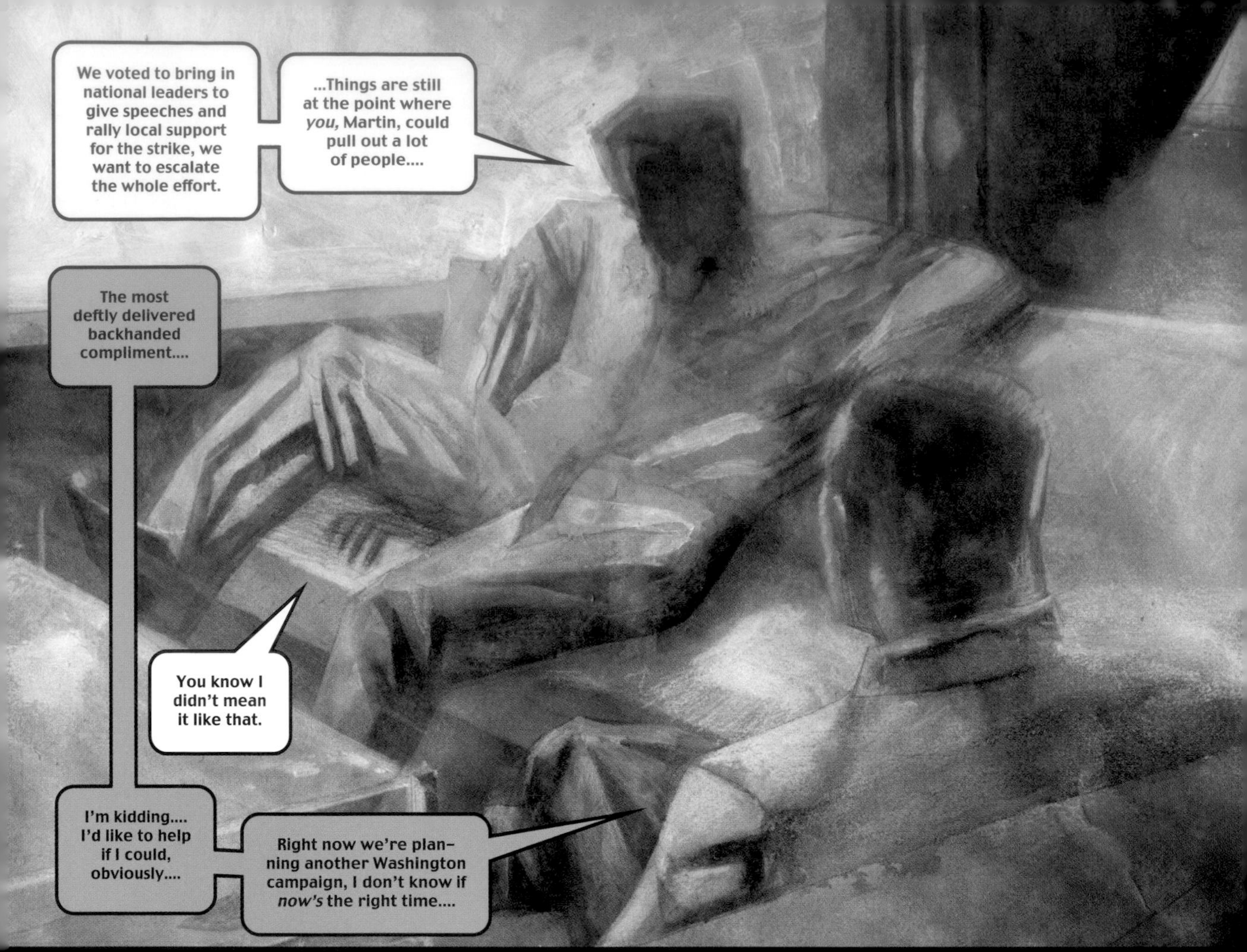
We voted to bring in national leaders to give speeches and rally local support for the strike, we want to escalate the whole effort.
...Things are still at the point where *you,* Martin, could pull out a lot of people....
The most deftly delivered backhanded compliment....
You know I didn't mean it like that.
I'm kidding.... I'd like to help if I could, obviously....
Right now we're plan-ning another Washington campaign, I don't know if *now's* the right time....

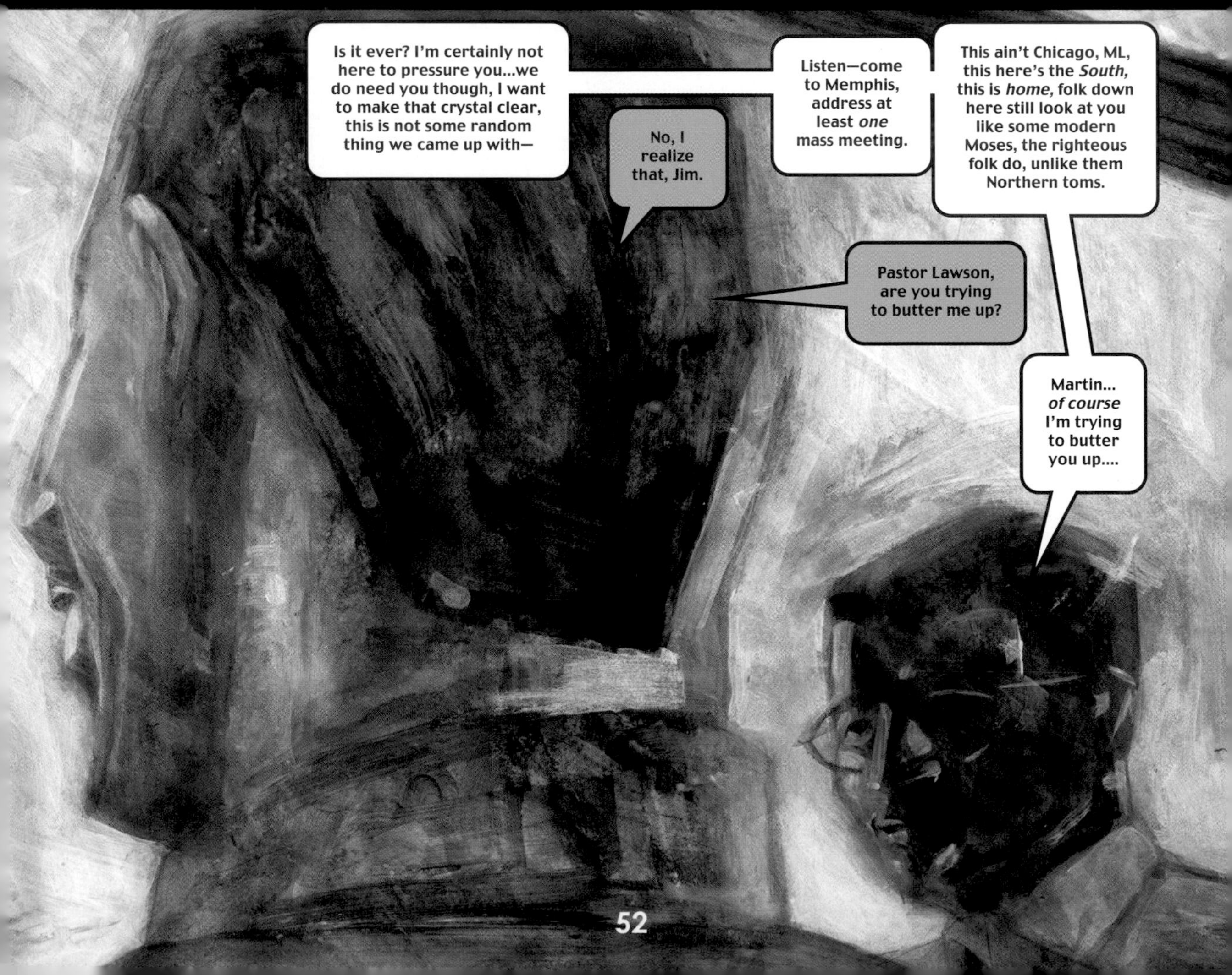
Is it ever? I'm certainly not here to pressure you...we do need you though, I want to make that crystal clear, this is not some random thing we came up with—
No, I realize that, Jim.
Listen—come to Memphis, address at least *one* mass meeting.
This ain't Chicago, ML, this here's the *South,* this is *home,* folk down here still look at you like some modern Moses, the righteous folk do, unlike them Northern toms.
Pastor Lawson, are you trying to butter me up?
Martin... *of course* I'm trying to butter you up....

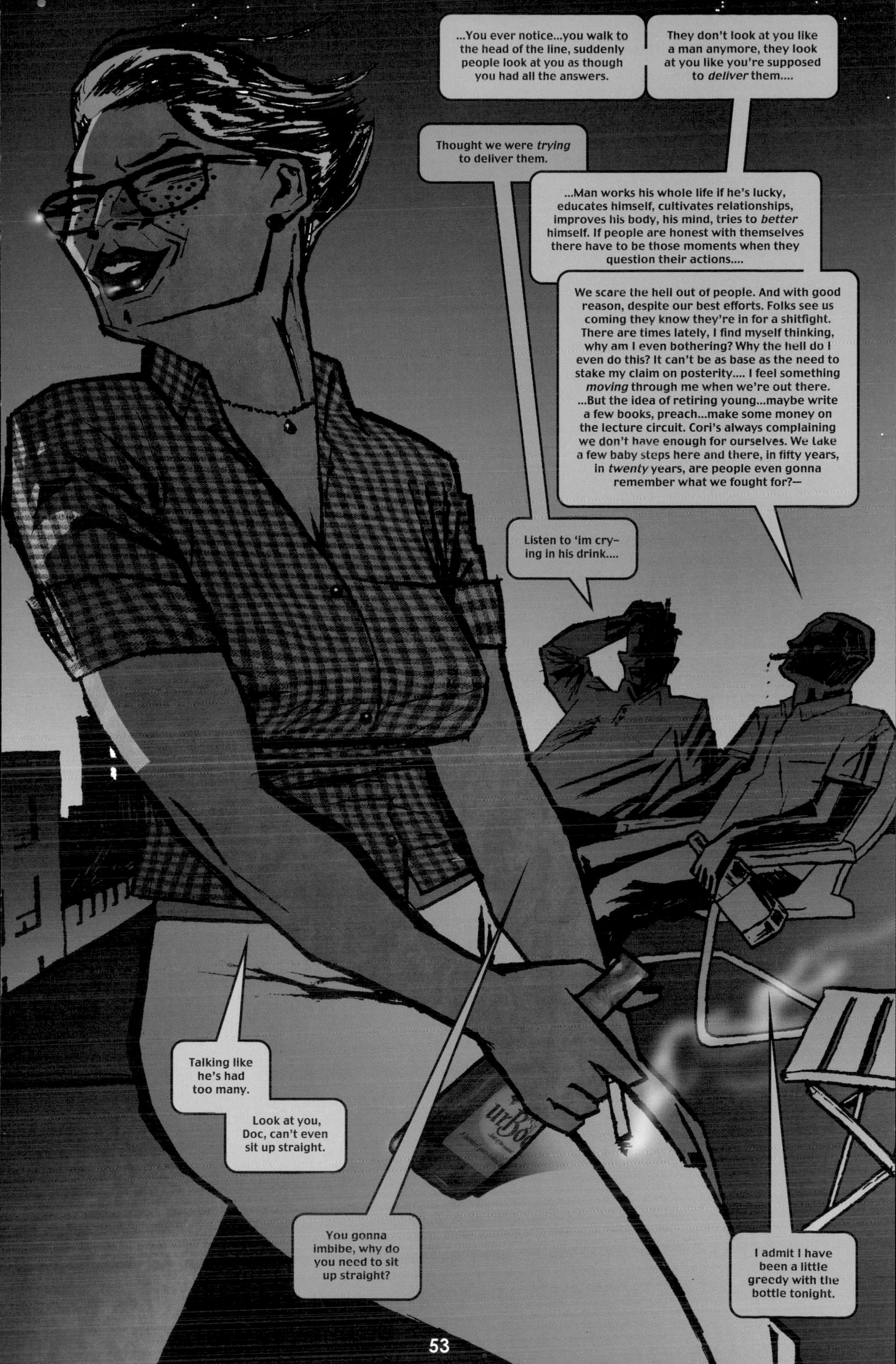
...You ever notice...you walk to the head of the line, suddenly people look at you as though you had all the answers.
They don't look at you like a man anymore, they look at you like you're supposed to *deliver* them....
Thought we were *trying* to deliver them.
...Man works his whole life if he's lucky, educates himself, cultivates relationships, improves his body, his mind, tries to *better* himself. If people are honest with themselves there have to be those moments when they question their actions....
We scare the hell out of people. And with good reason, despite our best efforts. Folks see us coming they know they're in for a shitfight. There are times lately, I find myself thinking, why am I even bothering? Why the hell do I even do this? It can't be as base as the need to stake my claim on posterity.... I feel something *moving* through me when we're out there. ...But the idea of retiring young...maybe write a few books, preach...make some money on the lecture circuit. Cori's always complaining we don't have enough for ourselves. We take a few baby steps here and there, in fifty years, in *twenty* years, are people even gonna remember what we fought for?—
Listen to 'im cry-ing in his drink....
Talking like he's had too many.
Look at you, Doc, can't even sit up straight.
You gonna imbibe, why do you need to sit up straight?
I admit I have been a little greedy with the bottle tonight.

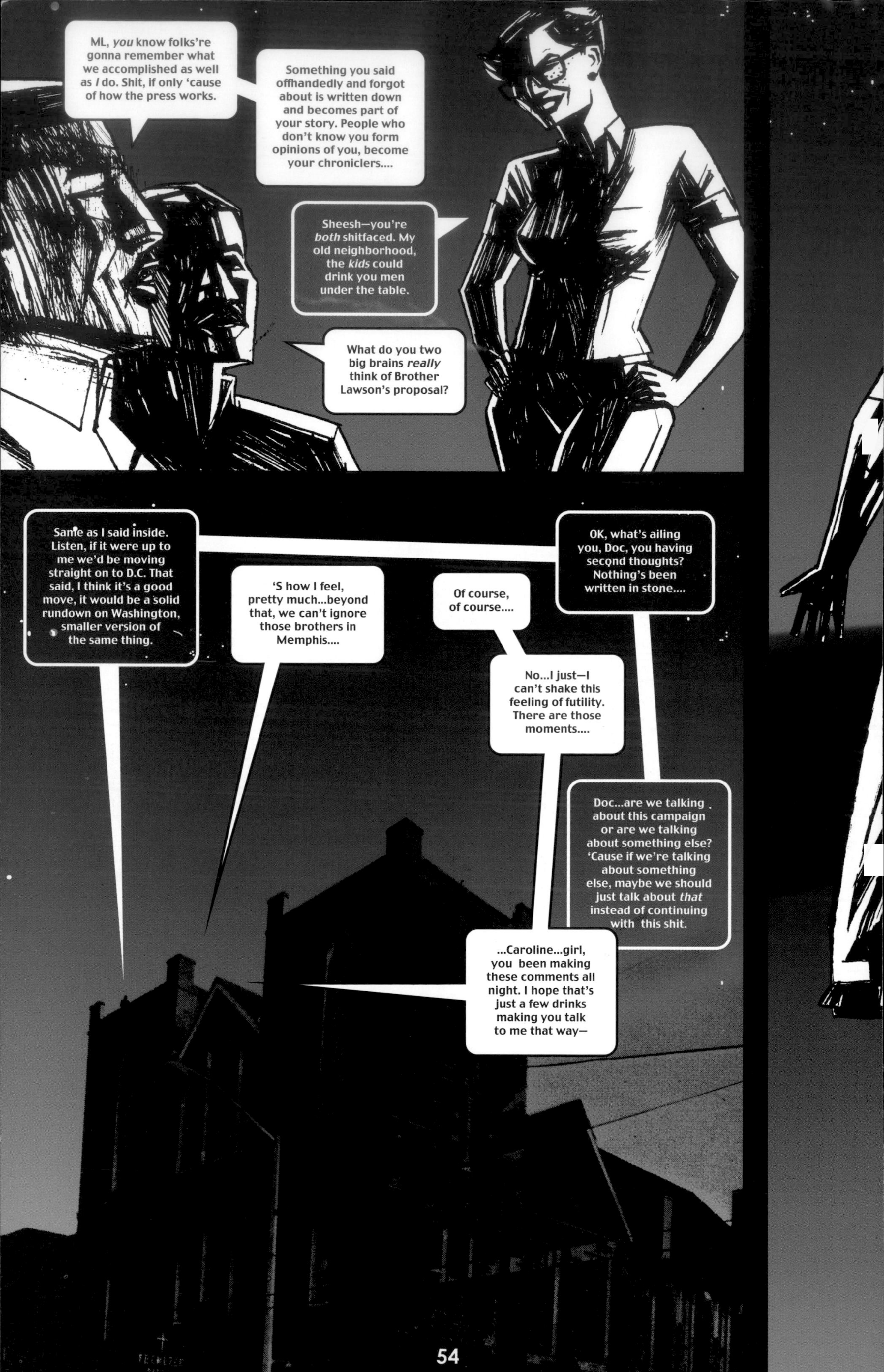
ML, *you* know folks're gonna remember what we accomplished as well as *I* do. Shit, if only 'cause of how the press works.
Something you said offhandedly and forgot about is written down and becomes part of your story. People who don't know you form opinions of you, become your chroniclers....
Sheesh—you're *both* shitfaced. My old neighborhood, the *kids* could drink you men under the table.
What do you two big brains *really* think of Brother Lawson's proposal?
Same as I said inside. Listen, if it were up to me we'd be moving straight on to D.C. That said, I think it's a good move, it would be a solid rundown on Washington, smaller version of the same thing.
'S how I feel, pretty much...beyond that, we can't ignore those brothers in Memphis....
Of course, of course....
OK, what's ailing you, Doc, you having second thoughts? Nothing's been written in stone....
No...I just—I can't shake this feeling of futility. There are those moments....
Doc...are we talking about this campaign or are we talking about something else? 'Cause if we're talking about something else, maybe we should just talk about *that* instead of continuing with this shit.
...Caroline...girl, you been making these comments all night. I hope that's just a few drinks making you talk to me that way—

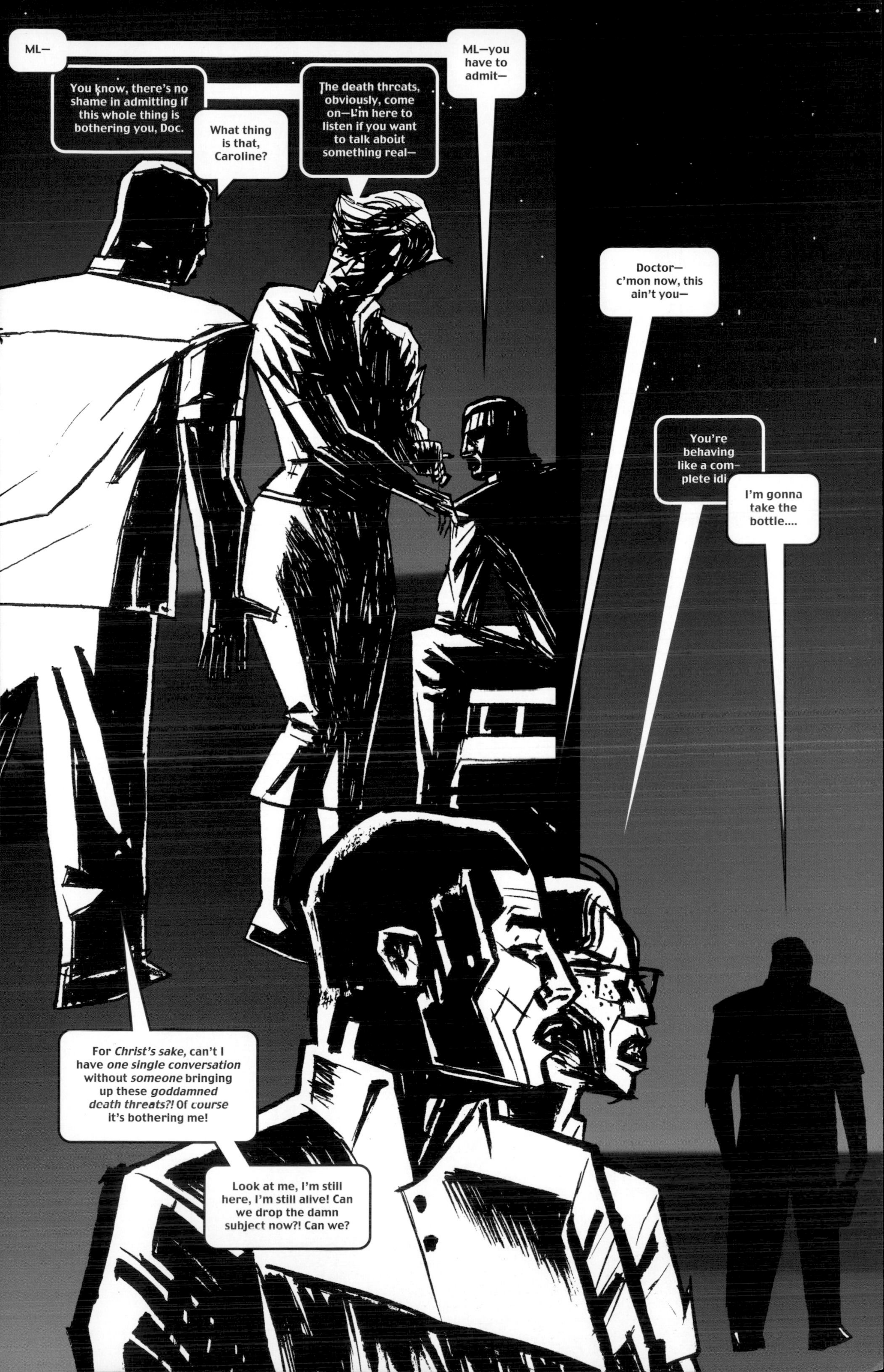
ML—
ML—you have to admit—
You know, there's no shame in admitting if this whole thing is bothering you, Doc.
What thing is that, Caroline?
The death threats, obviously, come on—I'm here to listen if you want to talk about something real—
Doctor— c'mon now, this ain't you—
You're behaving like a com-plete idi
I'm gonna take the bottle....
For *Christ's sake,* can't I have *one single conversation* without *someone* bringing up these *goddamned death threats?!* Of *course* it's bothering me!
Look at me, I'm still here, I'm still alive! Can we drop the damn subject now?! Can we?

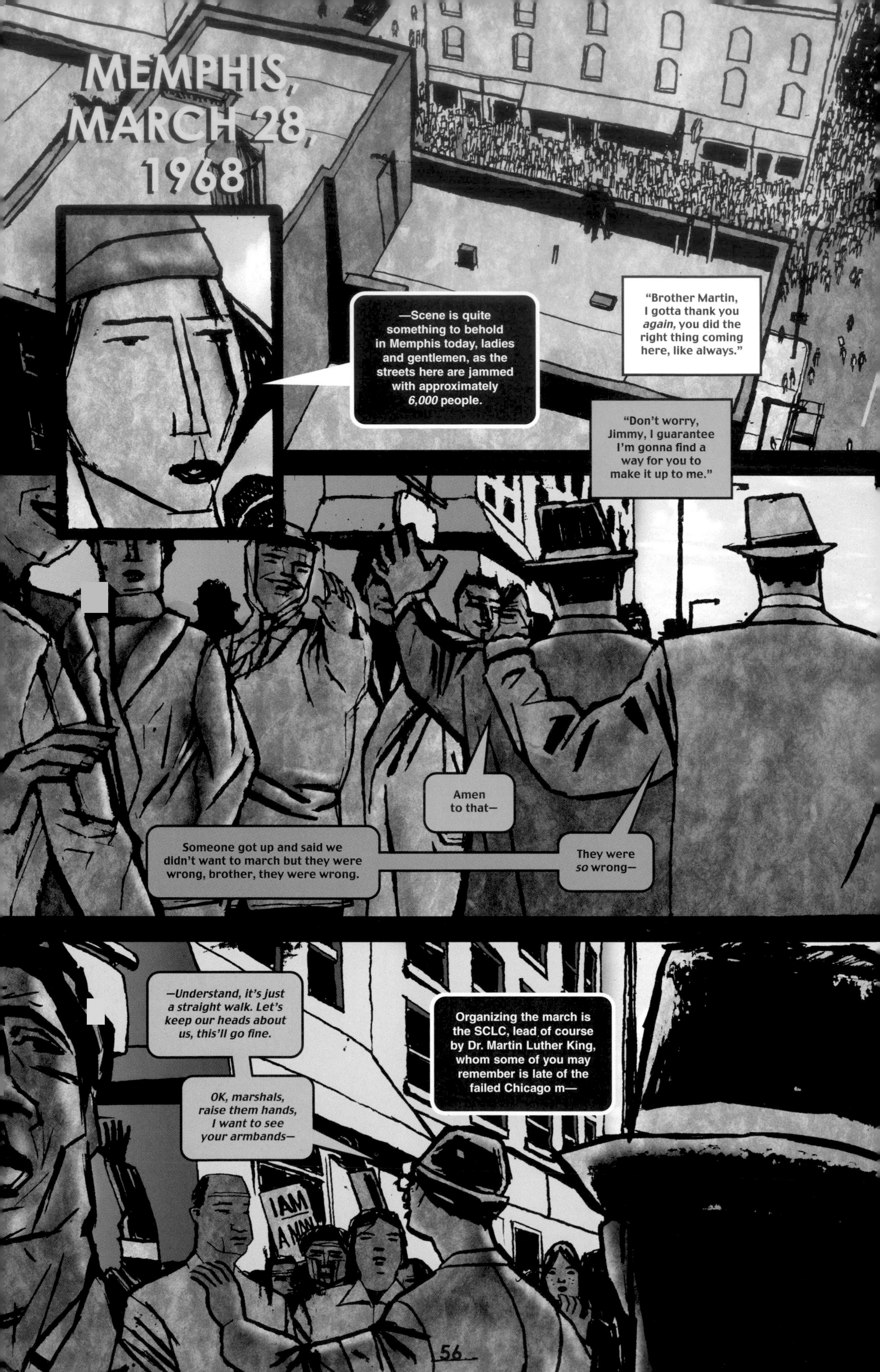
MEMPHIS, MARCH 28, 1968
—Scene is quite something to behold in Memphis today, ladies and gentlemen, as the streets here are jammed with approximately *6,000* people.
"Brother Martin, I gotta thank you *again,* you did the right thing coming here, like always."
"Don't worry, Jimmy, I guarantee I'm gonna find a way for you to make it up to me."
Amen to that—
Someone got up and said we didn't want to march but they were wrong, brother, they were wrong.
They were *so* wrong—
—Understand, it's just a straight walk. Let's keep our heads about us, this'll go fine.
OK, marshals, raise them hands, I want to see your armbands—
Organizing the march is the SCLC, lead of course by Dr. Martin Luther King, whom some of you may remember is late of the failed Chicago m—
I AM A MAN

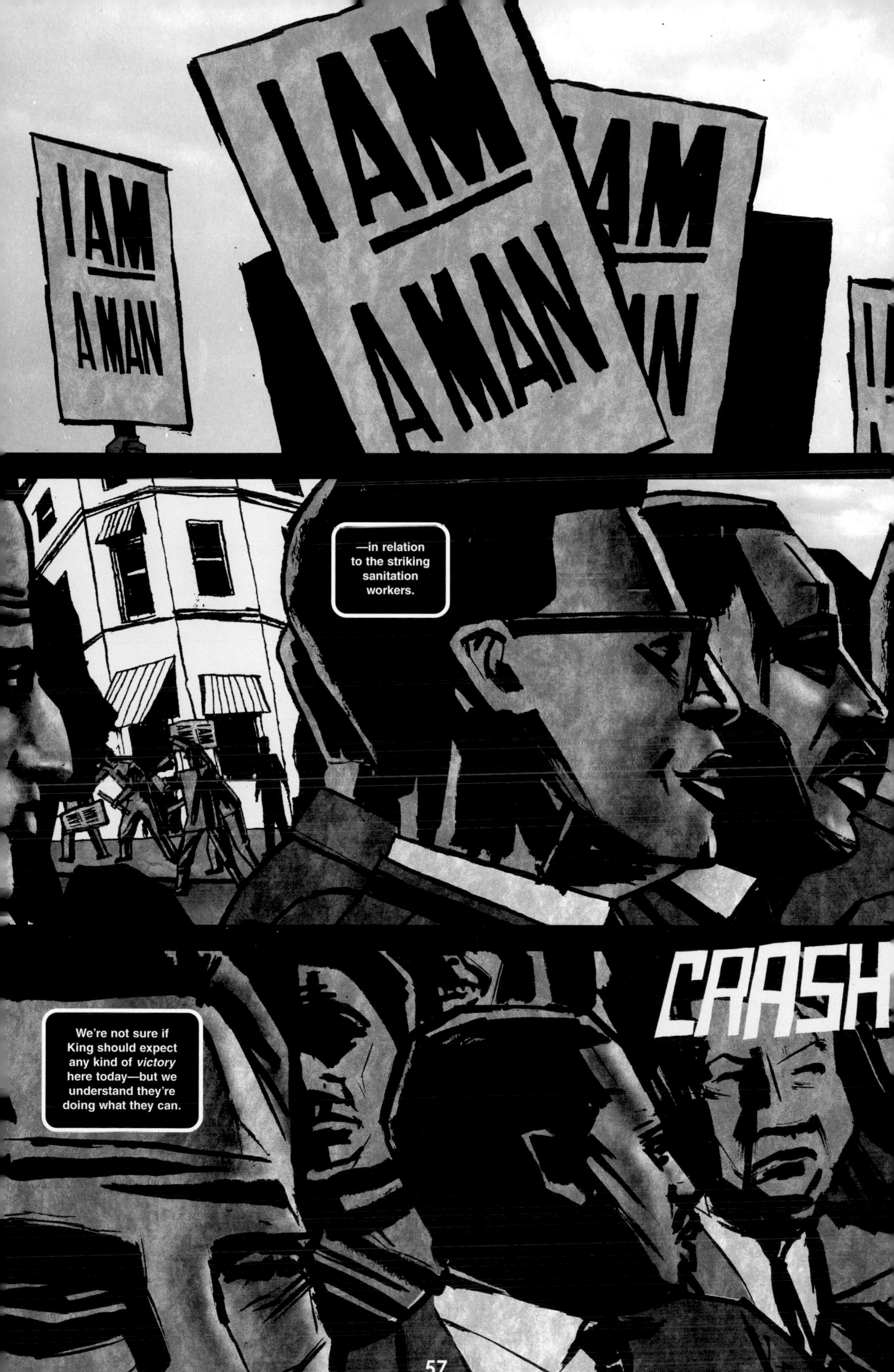
I AM A MAN
I AM A MAN
AM
—in relation to the striking sanitation workers.
We're not sure if King should expect any kind of *victory* here today—but we understand they're doing what they can.
CRASH

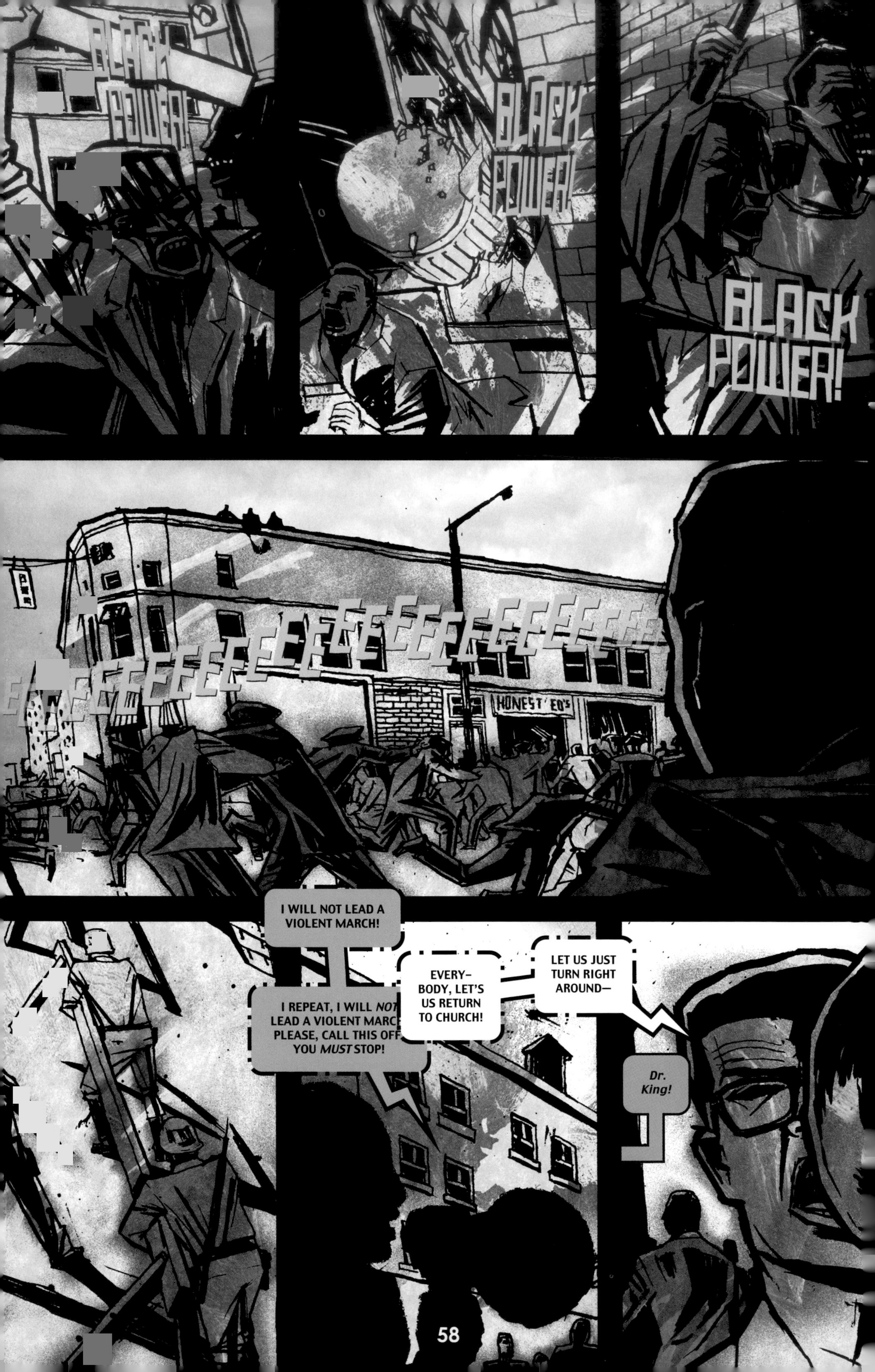
BLACK POWER!
BLACK POWER!
BLACK POWER!
EEEEEEEEEEEEEEEEEEEE
HONEST ED's
I WILL NOT LEAD A VIOLENT MARCH!
I REPEAT, I WILL *NOT* LEAD A VIOLENT MARC PLEASE, CALL THIS OFF YOU *MUST* STOP!
EVERY-BODY, LET'S US RETURN TO CHURCH!
LET US JUST TURN RIGHT AROUND—
Dr. King!

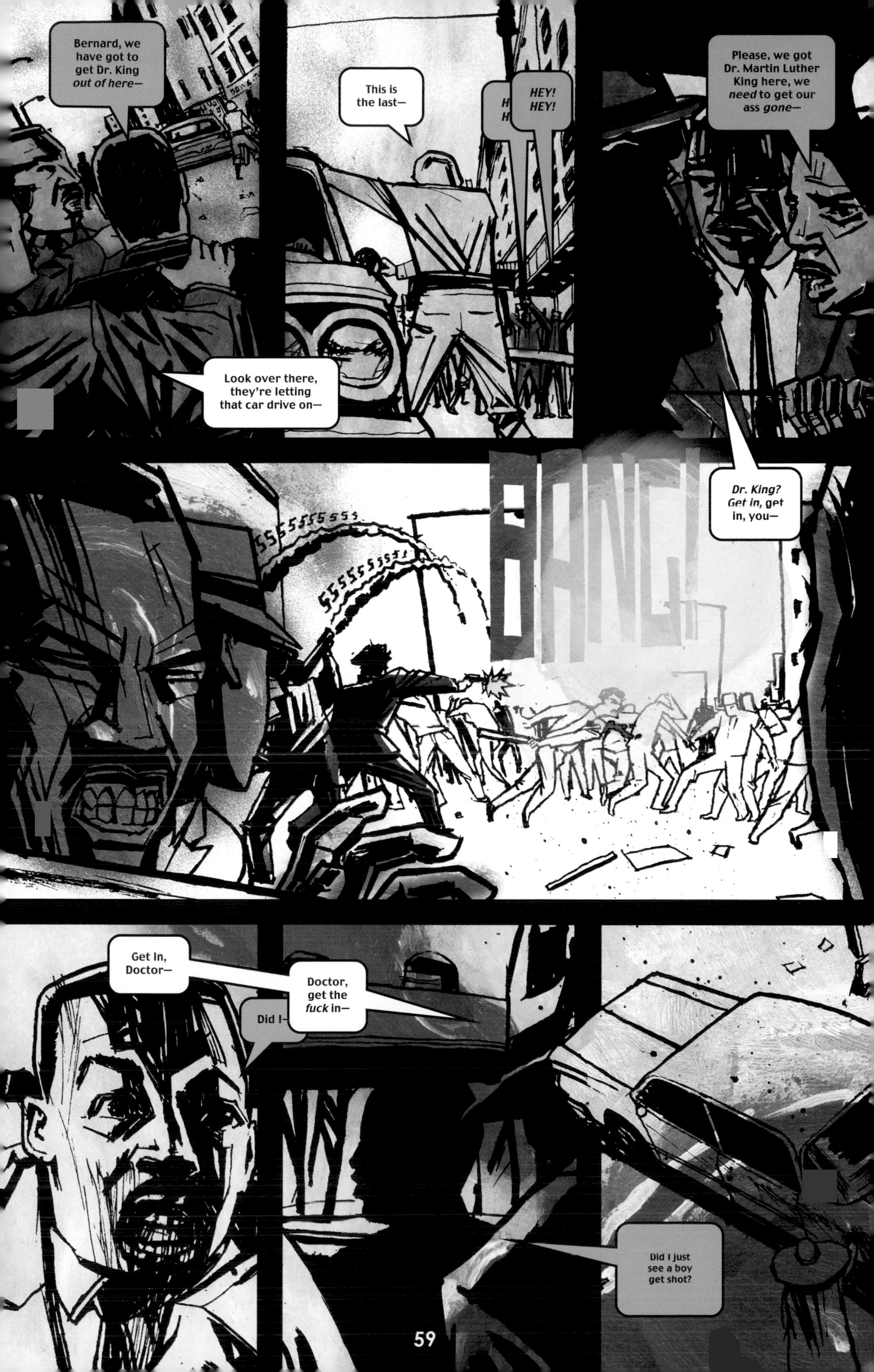

Bernard, we have got to get Dr. King *out of here*—
This is the last—
HEY! HEY!
Please, we got Dr. Martin Luther King here, we *need* to get our ass *gone*—
Look over there, they're letting that car drive on—
BANG!
Dr. King? Get in, get in, you—
Get In, Doctor—
Did I—
Doctor, get the *fuck* in—
Did I just see a boy get shot?

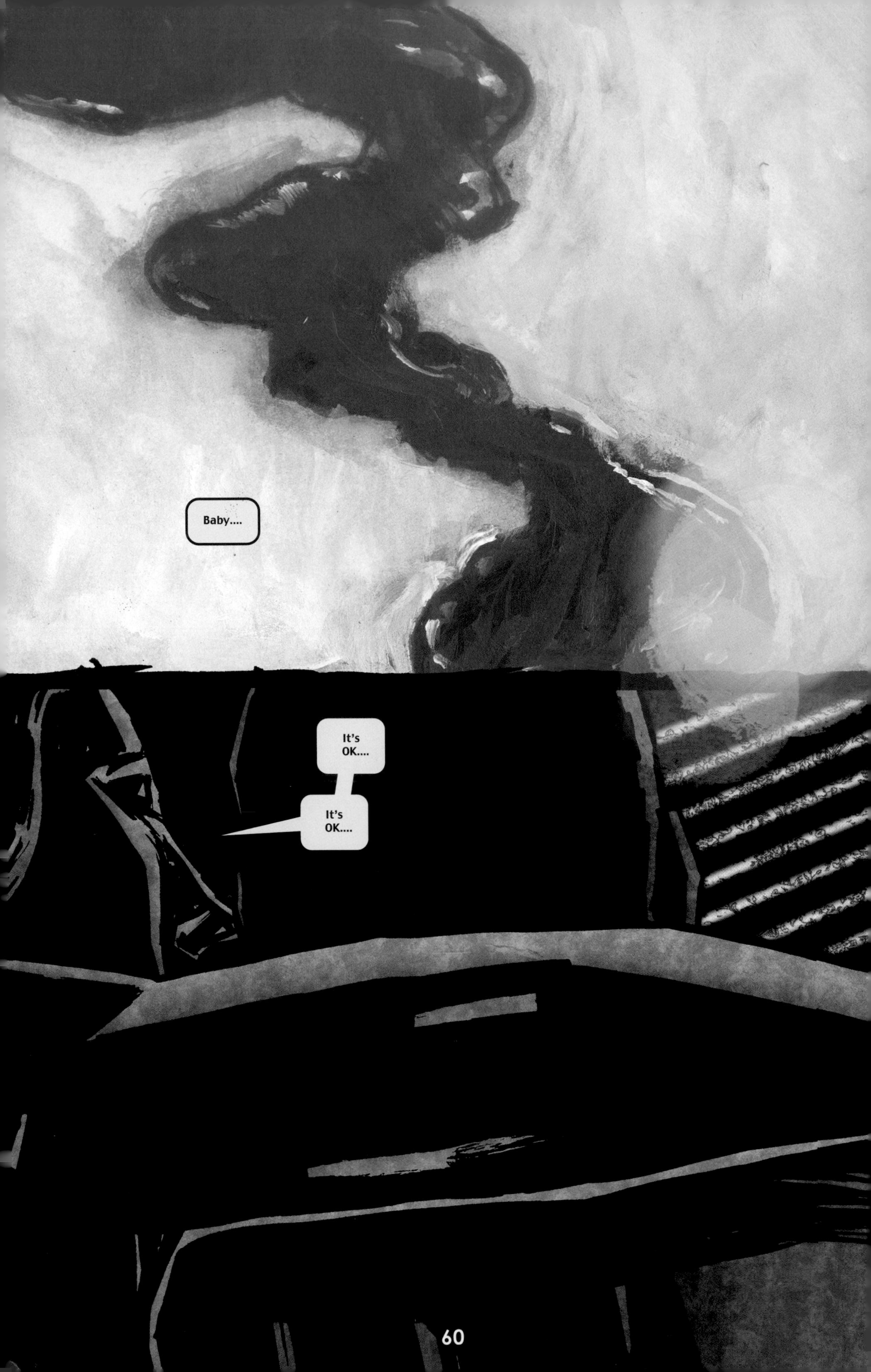
Baby....
It's OK....
It's OK....

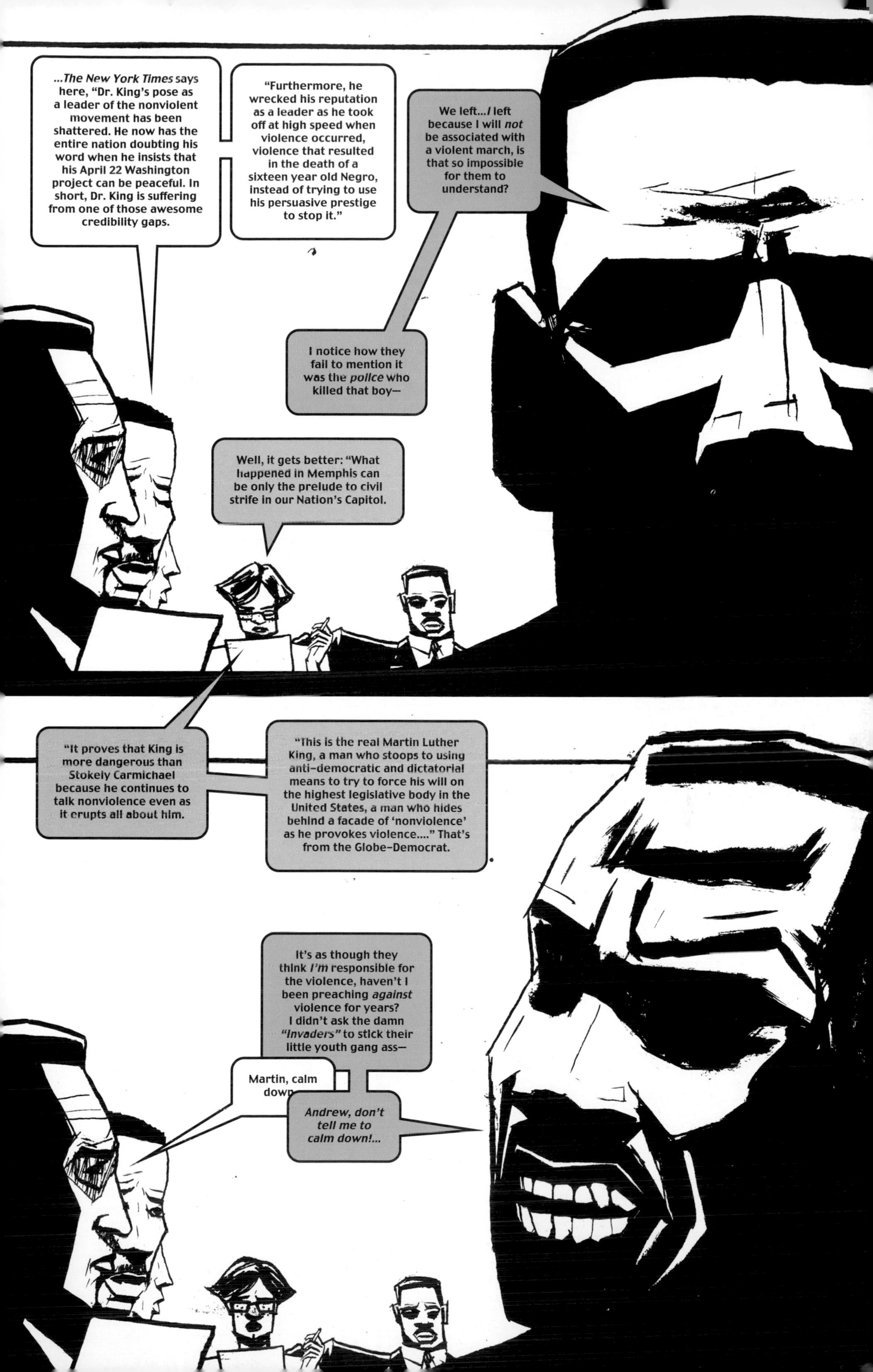
...*The New York Times* says here, "Dr. King's pose as a leader of the nonviolent movement has been shattered. He now has the entire nation doubting his word when he insists that his April 22 Washington project can be peaceful. In short, Dr. King is suffering from one of those awesome credibility gaps.
"Furthermore, he wrecked his reputation as a leader as he took off at high speed when violence occurred, violence that resulted in the death of a sixteen year old Negro, instead of trying to use his persuasive prestige to stop it."
We left...*I* left because I will *not* be associated with a violent march, is that so impossible for them to understand?
I notice how they fail to mention it was the *police* who killed that boy—
Well, it gets better: "What happened in Memphis can be only the prelude to civil strife in our Nation's Capitol.
"It proves that King is more dangerous than Stokely Carmichael because he continues to talk nonviolence even as it erupts all about him.
"This is the real Martin Luther King, a man who stoops to using anti-democratic and dictatorial means to try to force his will on the highest legislative body in the United States, a man who hides behind a facade of 'nonviolence' as he provokes violence...." That's from the Globe-Democrat.
It's as though they think *I'm* responsible for the violence, haven't I been preaching *against* violence for years? I didn't ask the damn *"Invaders"* to stick their little youth gang ass—
Martin, calm down
Andrew, don't tell me to calm down!...

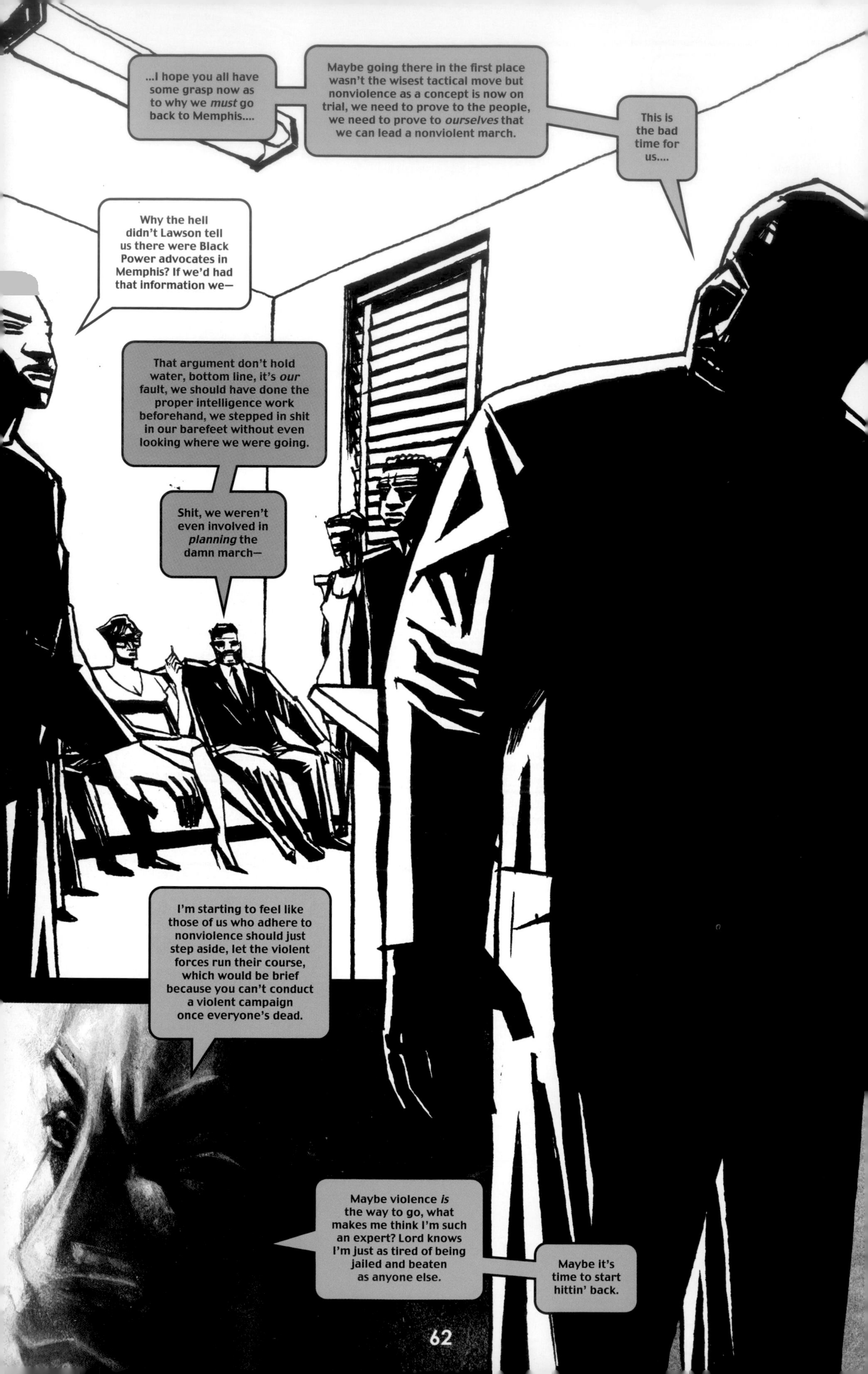
...I hope you all have some grasp now as to why we *must* go back to Memphis....
Maybe going there in the first place wasn't the wisest tactical move but nonviolence as a concept is now on trial, we need to prove to the people, we need to prove to *ourselves* that we can lead a nonviolent march.
This is the bad time for us....
Why the hell didn't Lawson tell us there were Black Power advocates in Memphis? If we'd had that information we—
That argument don't hold water, bottom line, it's *our* fault, we should have done the proper intelligence work beforehand, we stepped in shit in our barefeet without even looking where we were going.
Shit, we weren't even involved in *planning* the damn march—
I'm starting to feel like those of us who adhere to nonviolence should just step aside, let the violent forces run their course, which would be brief because you can't conduct a violent campaign once everyone's dead.
Maybe violence *is* the way to go, what makes me think I'm such an expert? Lord knows I'm just as tired of being jailed and beaten as anyone else.
Maybe it's time to start hittin' back.

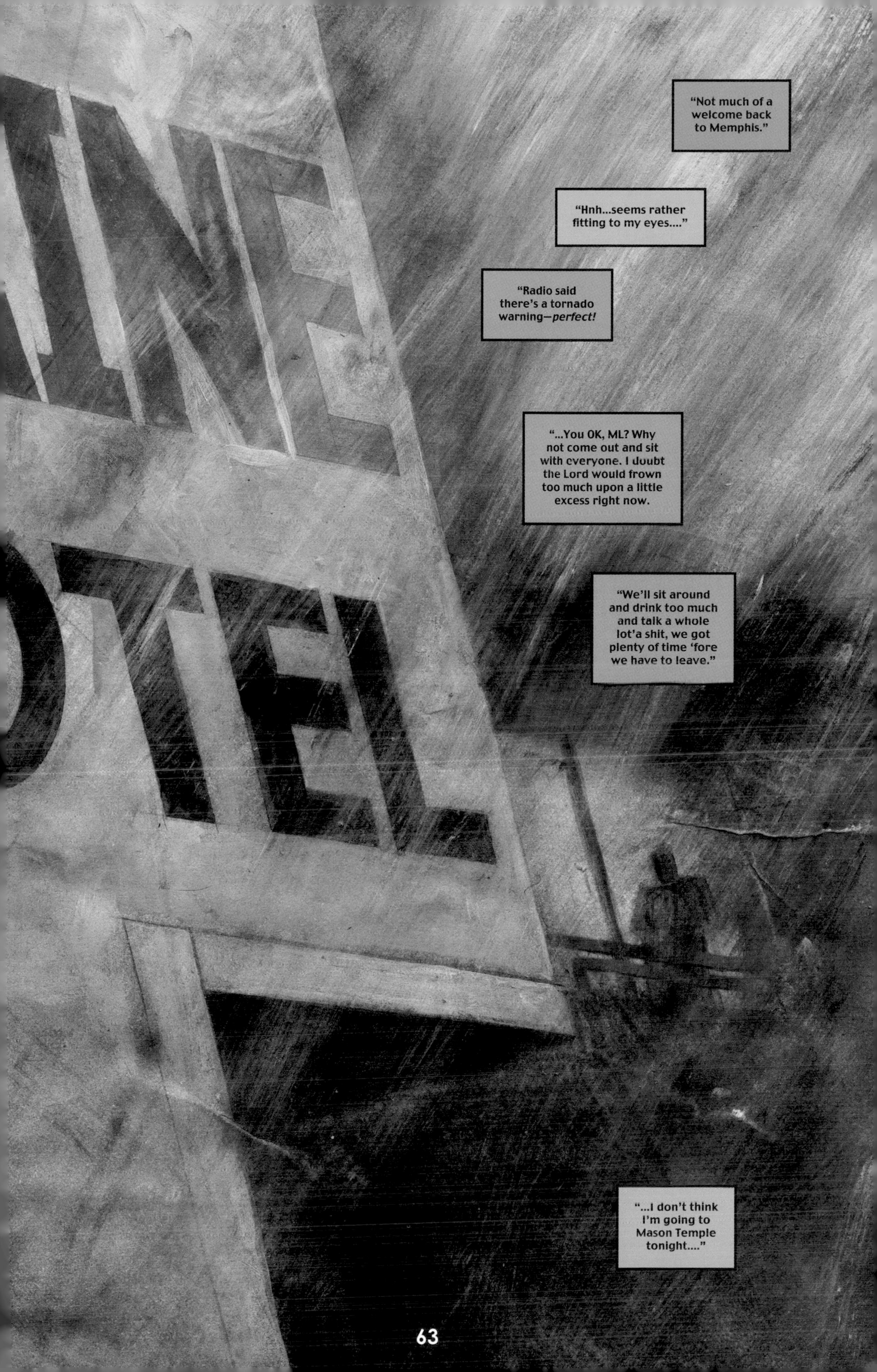
"Not much of a welcome back to Memphis."
"Hnh...seems rather fitting to my eyes...."
"Radio said there's a tornado warning—*perfect!*
"...You OK, ML? Why not come out and sit with everyone. I doubt the Lord would frown too much upon a little excess right now.
"We'll sit around and drink too much and talk a whole lot'a shit, we got plenty of time 'fore we have to leave."
"...I don't think I'm going to Mason Temple tonight...."

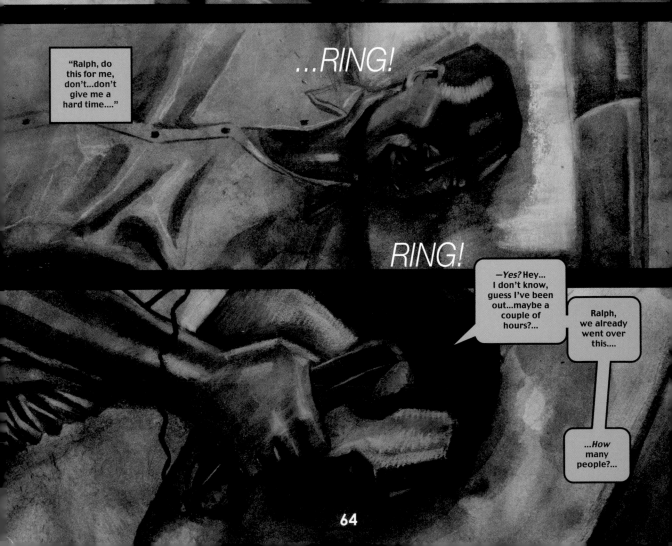

"...Why do you say?"

"No one would be fool enough to show up in this. You said yourself there's a tornado warning...."

"Getting too used to them big ass crowds."

"I suppose you want me to speak for you. You realize how often you've been ducking out of speeches lately?, using me as your stand-in...."

"You worried if folks don't come the press is gonna say no one wants to hear you speak?"

"I didn't say that...."

"Ralph, do this for me, don't...don't give me a hard time...."

...RING!

RING!

—Yes? Hey... I don't know, guess I've been out...maybe a couple of hours?...

Ralph, we already went over this....

...How many people?...

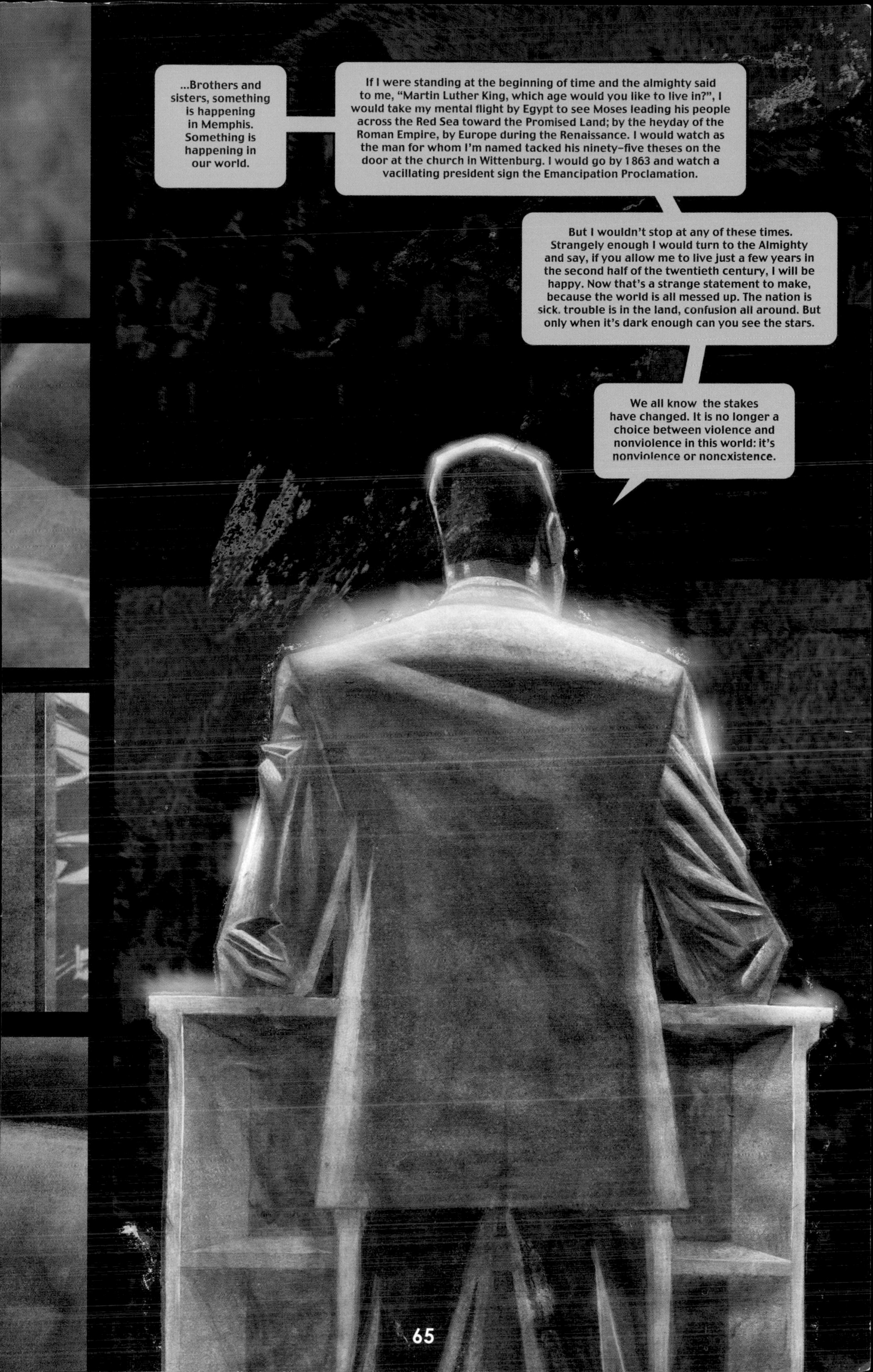
...Brothers and sisters, something is happening in Memphis. Something is happening in our world.
If I were standing at the beginning of time and the almighty said to me, "Martin Luther King, which age would you like to live in?", I would take my mental flight by Egypt to see Moses leading his people across the Red Sea toward the Promised Land; by the heyday of the Roman Empire, by Europe during the Renaissance. I would watch as the man for whom I'm named tacked his ninety-five theses on the door at the church in Wittenburg. I would go by 1863 and watch a vacillating president sign the Emancipation Proclamation.
But I wouldn't stop at any of these times. Strangely enough I would turn to the Almighty and say, if you allow me to live just a few years in the second half of the twentieth century, I will be happy. Now that's a strange statement to make, because the world is all messed up. The nation is sick. trouble is in the land, confusion all around. But only when it's dark enough can you see the stars.
We all know the stakes have changed. It is no longer a choice between violence and nonviolence in this world: it's nonviolence or nonexistence.

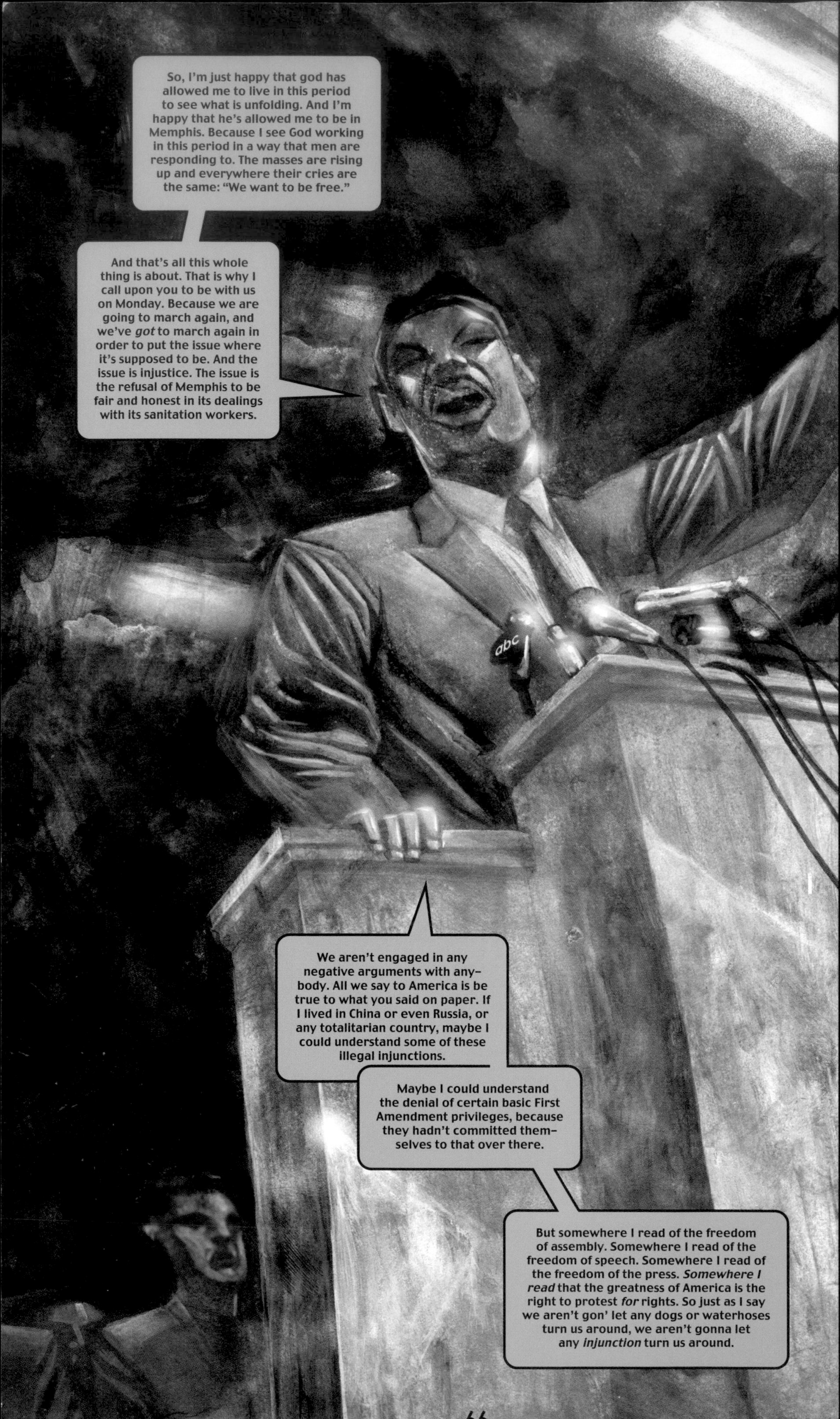
So, I'm just happy that god has allowed me to live in this period to see what is unfolding. And I'm happy that he's allowed me to be in Memphis. Because I see God working in this period in a way that men are responding to. The masses are rising up and everywhere their cries are the same: "We want to be free."
And that's all this whole thing is about. That is why I call upon you to be with us on Monday. Because we are going to march again, and we've *got* to march again in order to put the issue where it's supposed to be. And the issue is injustice. The issue is the refusal of Memphis to be fair and honest in its dealings with its sanitation workers.
abc
We aren't engaged in any negative arguments with any-body. All we say to America is be true to what you said on paper. If I lived in China or even Russia, or any totalitarian country, maybe I could understand some of these illegal injunctions.
Maybe I could understand the denial of certain basic First Amendment privileges, because they hadn't committed them-selves to that over there.
But somewhere I read of the freedom of assembly. Somewhere I read of the freedom of speech. Somewhere I read of the freedom of the press. *Somewhere I read* that the greatness of America is the right to protest *for* rights. So just as I say we aren't gon' let any dogs or waterhoses turn us around, we aren't gonna let any *injunction* turn us around.

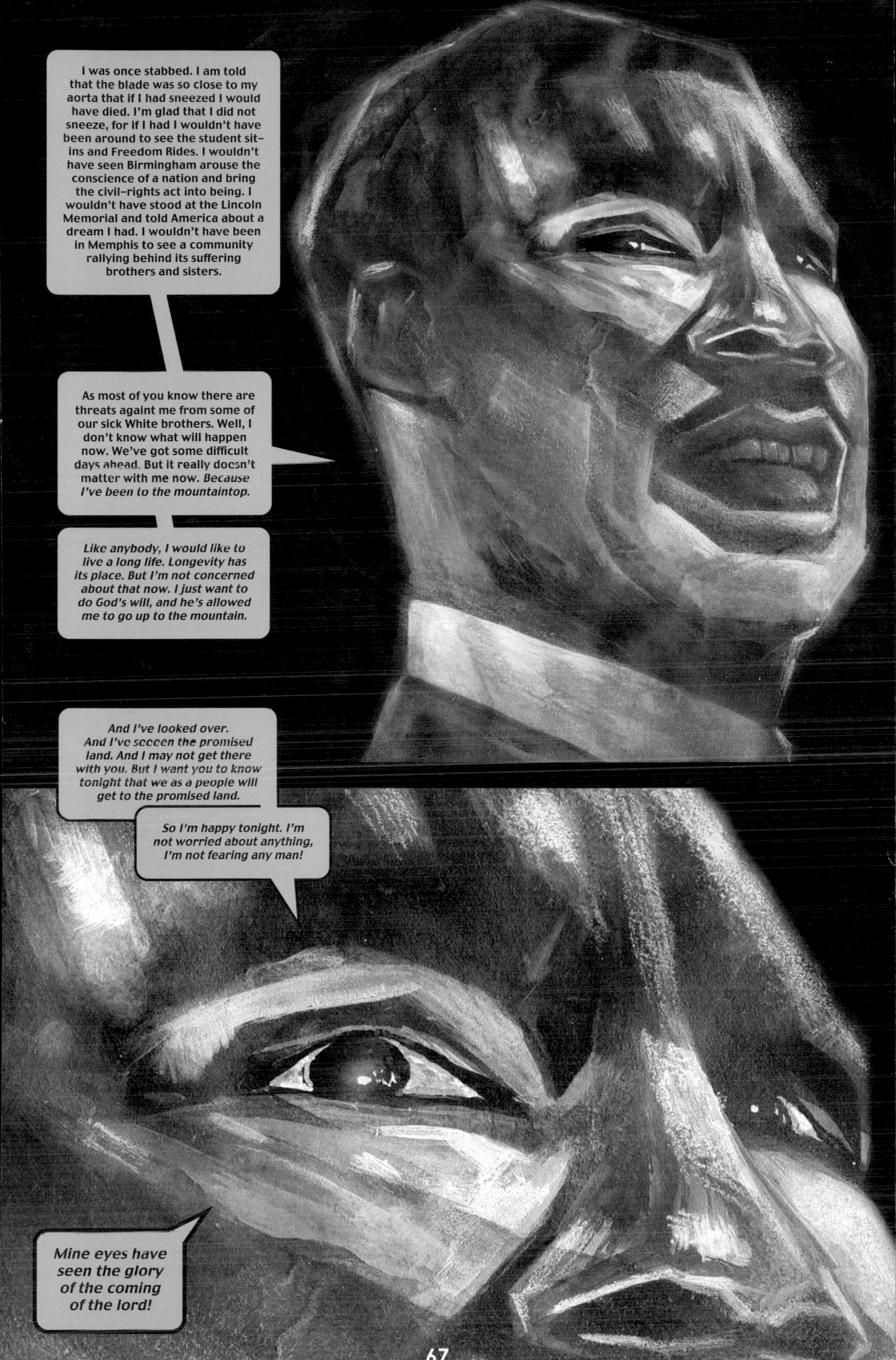
I was once stabbed. I am told that the blade was so close to my aorta that if I had sneezed I would have died. I'm glad that I did not sneeze, for if I had I wouldn't have been around to see the student sit-ins and Freedom Rides. I wouldn't have seen Birmingham arouse the conscience of a nation and bring the civil-rights act into being. I wouldn't have stood at the Lincoln Memorial and told America about a dream I had. I wouldn't have been in Memphis to see a community rallying behind its suffering brothers and sisters.
As most of you know there are threats againt me from some of our sick White brothers. Well, I don't know what will happen now. We've got some difficult days ahead. But it really doesn't matter with me now. Because I've been to the mountaintop.
Like anybody, I would like to live a long life. Longevity has its place. But I'm not concerned about that now. I just want to do God's will, and he's allowed me to go up to the mountain.
And I've looked over. And I've seeeen the promised land. And I may not get there with you. But I want you to know tonight that we as a people will get to the promised land.
So I'm happy tonight. I'm not worried about anything, I'm not fearing any man!
Mine eyes have seen the glory of the coming of the lord!

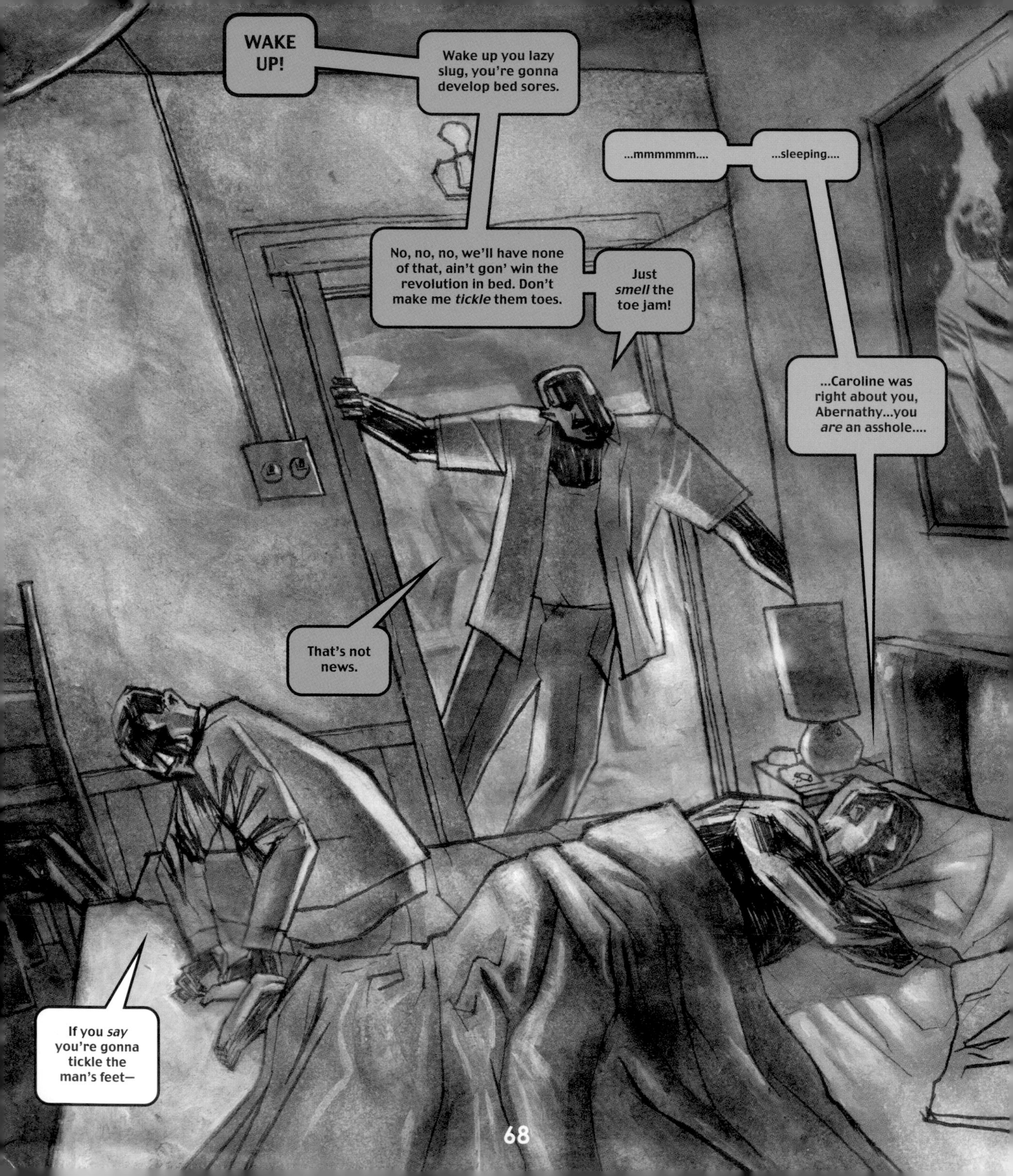
WAKE UP!
Wake up you lazy slug, you're gonna develop bed sores.
...mmmmmm....
...sleeping....
No, no, no, we'll have none of that, ain't gon' win the revolution in bed. Don't make me *tickle* them toes.
Just *smell* the toe jam!
...Caroline was right about you, Abernathy...you *are* an asshole....
That's not news.
If you *say* you're gonna tickle the man's feet—

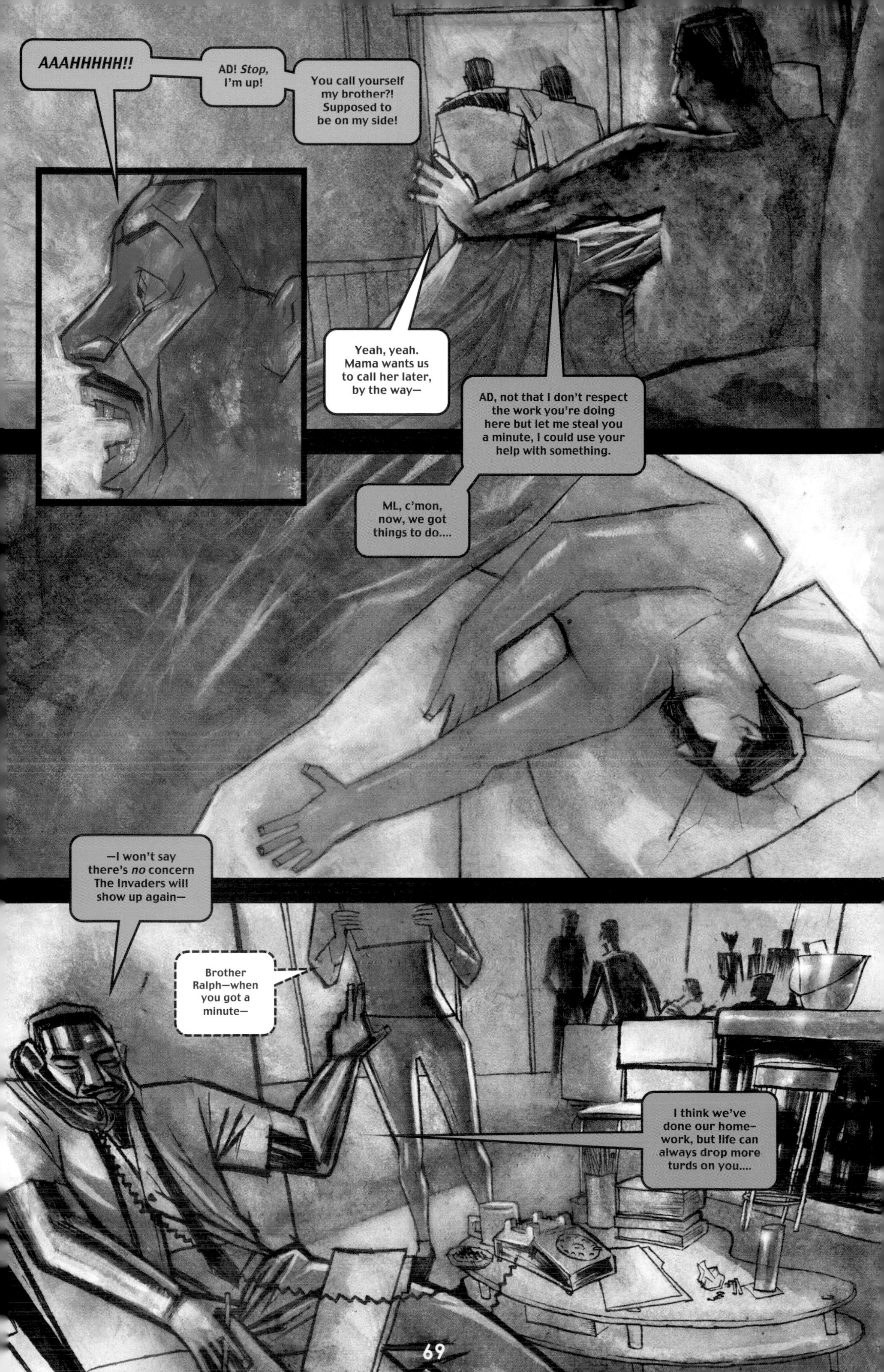
AAAHHHHH!!
AD! *Stop,* I'm up!
You call yourself my brother?! Supposed to be on my side!
Yeah, yeah. Mama wants us to call her later, by the way—
AD, not that I don't respect the work you're doing here but let me steal you a minute, I could use your help with something.
ML, c'mon, now, we got things to do....
—I won't say there's *no* concern The Invaders will show up again—
Brother Ralph—when you got a minute—
I think we've done our home-work, but life can always drop more turds on you....

THE
Welcome to
LORRAINE
MOTEL
302
304
202
204
Actually, Hosea's bringing one of them in later for a meeting, try and get them on-side for the march just in case—not really sure how ML's gonna react to that, so stay tuned.
"Oh, the cops are still out there—*and* the FBI, *real* discreet. I don't even think these boys are *tryin'* anymore.
"Yeah, he's good. Listen closely you can hear him singing in the shower, finally got his ass out of bed.

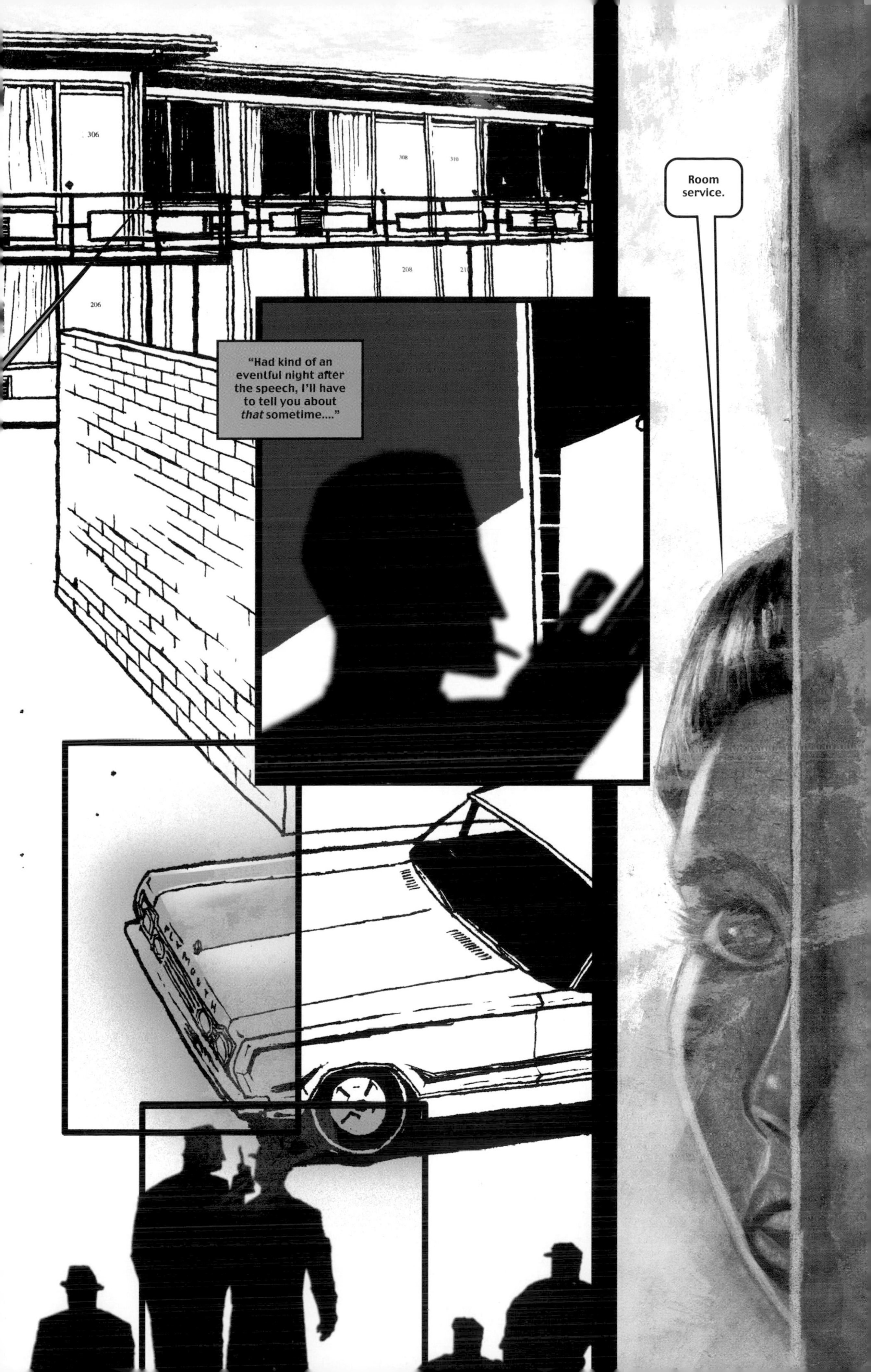

"Had kind of an eventful night after the speech, I'll have to tell you about *that* sometime...."
Room service.

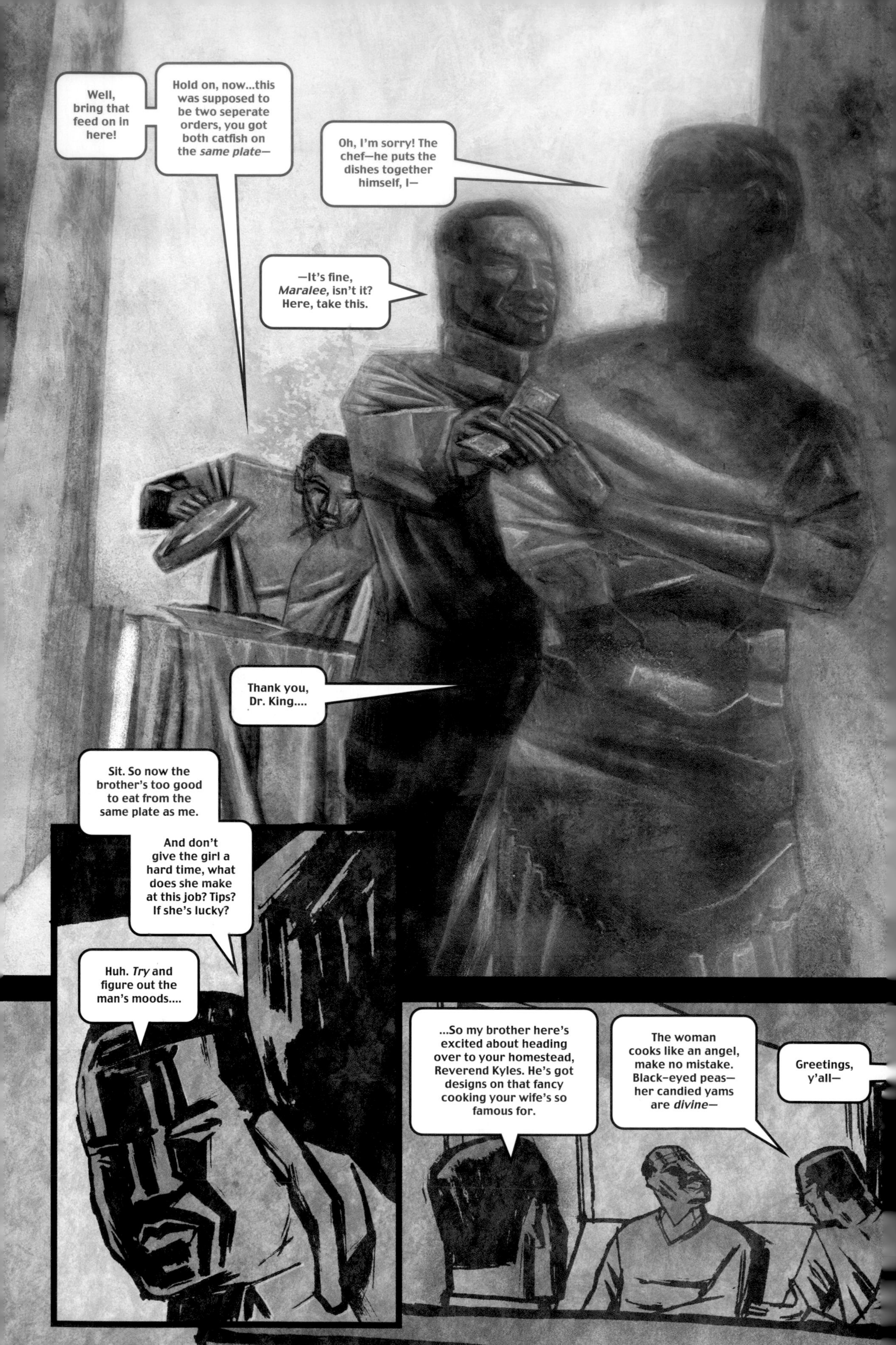
Well, bring that feed on in here!
Hold on, now...this was supposed to be two seperate orders, you got both catfish on the *same plate*—
Oh, I'm sorry! The chef—he puts the dishes together himself, I—
—It's fine, *Maralee*, isn't it? Here, take this.
Thank you, Dr. King....
Sit. So now the brother's too good to eat from the same plate as me.
And don't give the girl a hard time, what does she make at this job? Tips? If she's lucky?
Huh. *Try* and figure out the man's moods....
...So my brother here's excited about heading over to your homestead, Reverend Kyles. He's got designs on that fancy cooking your wife's so famous for.
The woman cooks like an angel, make no mistake. Black-eyed peas—her candied yams are *divine*—
Greetings, y'all—

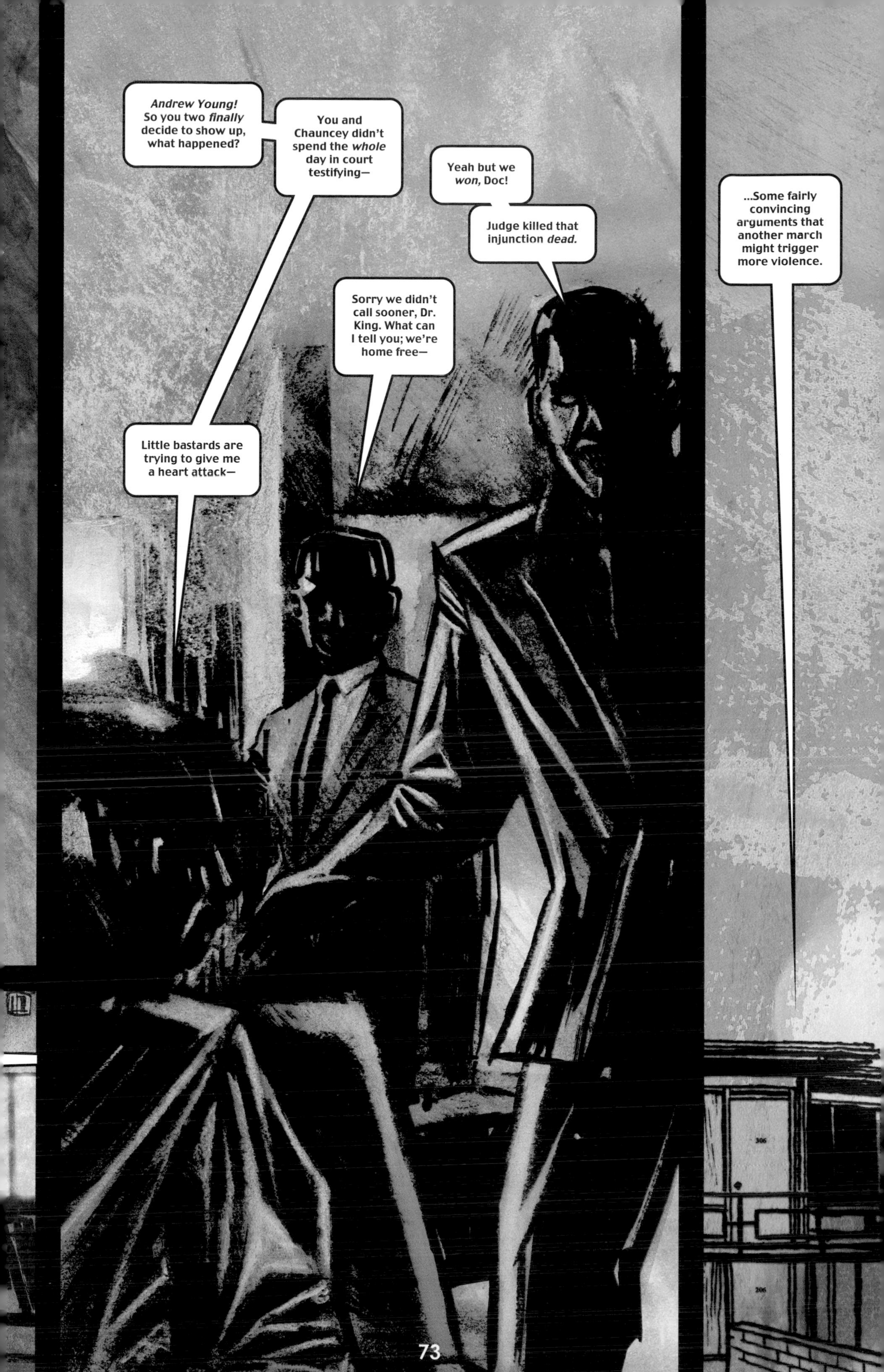
Andrew Young! So you two finally decide to show up, what happened?
You and Chauncey didn't spend the whole day in court testifying—
Little bastards are trying to give me a heart attack—
Sorry we didn't call sooner, Dr. King. What can I tell you; we're home free—
Yeah but we won, Doc!
Judge killed that injunction dead.
...Some fairly convincing arguments that another march might trigger more violence.
306
206

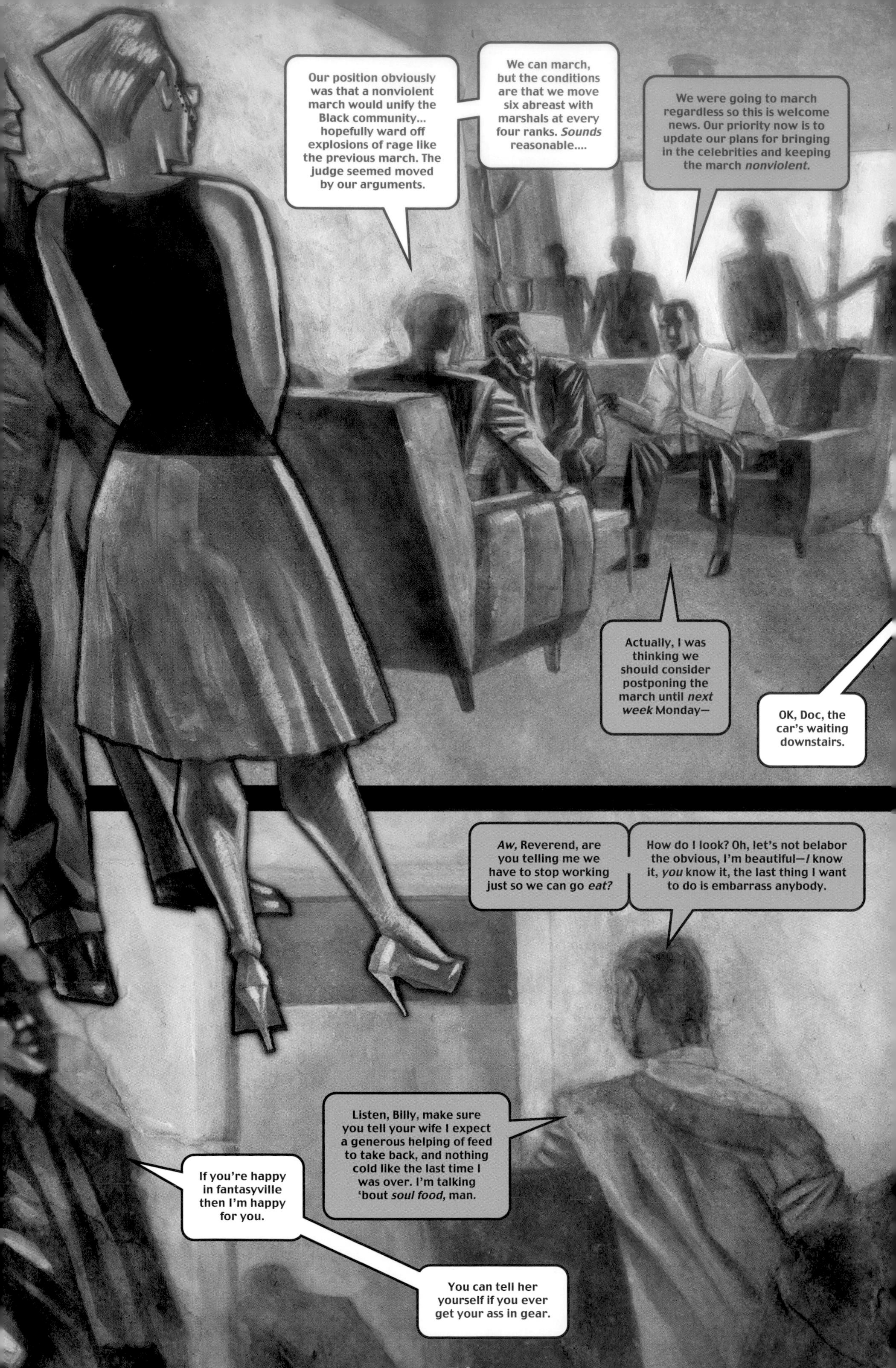
Our position obviously was that a nonviolent march would unify the Black community... hopefully ward off explosions of rage like the previous march. The judge seemed moved by our arguments.
We can march, but the conditions are that we move six abreast with marshals at every four ranks. *Sounds* reasonable....
We were going to march regardless so this is welcome news. Our priority now is to update our plans for bringing in the celebrities and keeping the march *nonviolent.*
Actually, I was thinking we should consider postponing the march until *next week* Monday—
OK, Doc, the car's waiting downstairs.
Aw, Reverend, are you telling me we have to stop working just so we can go *eat?*
How do I look? Oh, let's not belabor the obvious, I'm beautiful—*I* know it, *you* know it, the last thing I want to do is embarrass anybody.
Listen, Billy, make sure you tell your wife I expect a generous helping of feed to take back, and nothing cold like the last time I was over. I'm talking 'bout *soul food,* man.
If you're happy in fantasyville then I'm happy for you.
You can tell her yourself if you ever get your ass in gear.

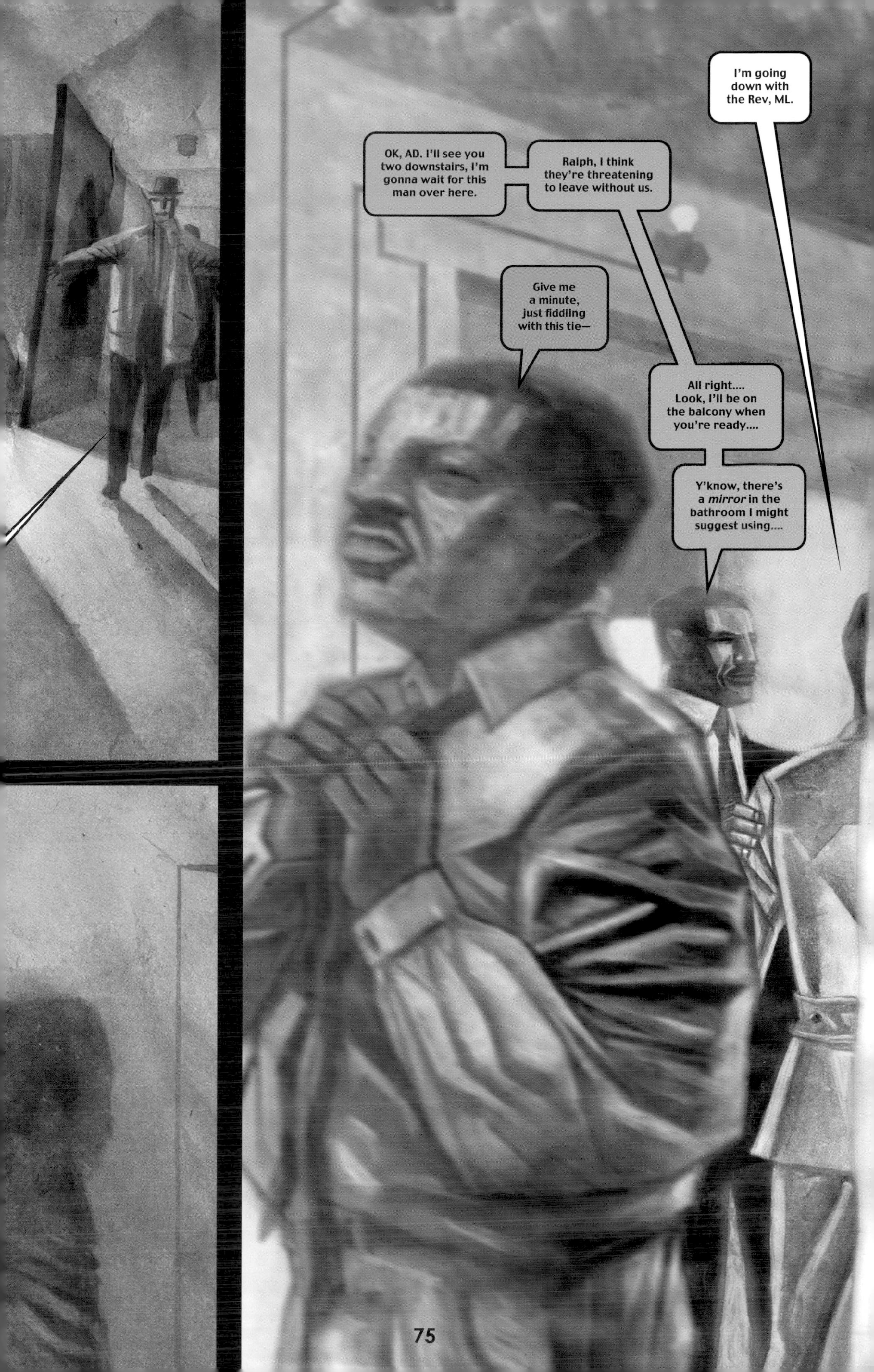
I'm going down with the Rev, ML.
OK, AD. I'll see you two downstairs, I'm gonna wait for this man over here.
Ralph, I think they're threatening to leave without us.
Give me a minute, just fiddling with this tie—
All right.... Look, I'll be on the balcony when you're ready....
Y'know, there's a *mirror* in the bathroom I might suggest using....

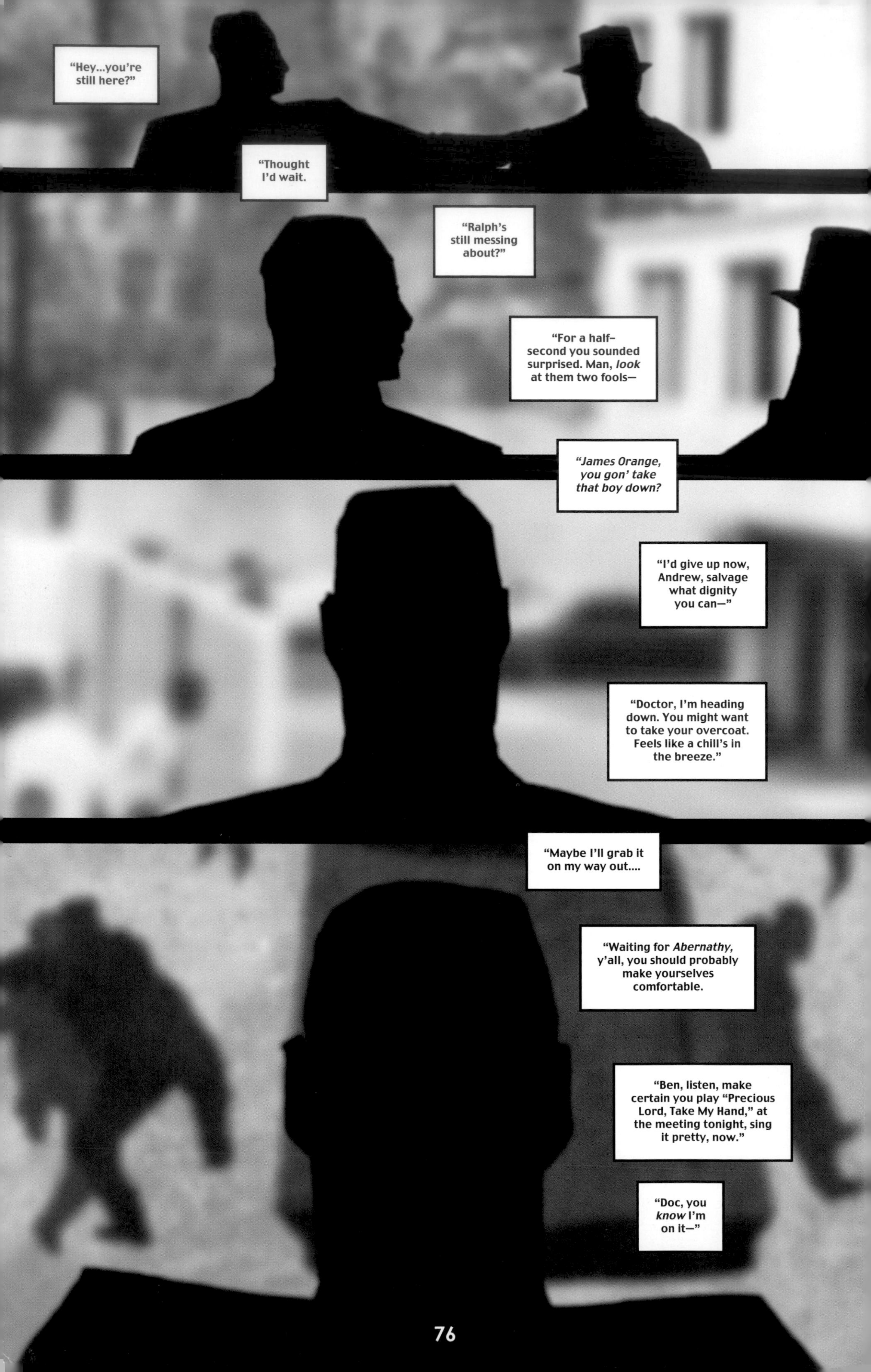
"Hey...you're still here?"
"Thought I'd wait.
"Ralph's still messing about?"
"For a half-second you sounded surprised. Man, *look* at them two fools—
"James Orange, you gon' take that boy down?
"I'd give up now, Andrew, salvage what dignity you can—"
"Doctor, I'm heading down. You might want to take your overcoat. Feels like a chill's in the breeze."
"Maybe I'll grab it on my way out....
"Waiting for *Abernathy,* y'all, you should probably make yourselves comfortable.
"Ben, listen, make certain you play "Precious Lord, Take My Hand," at the meeting tonight, sing it pretty, now."
"Doc, you *know* I'm on it—"

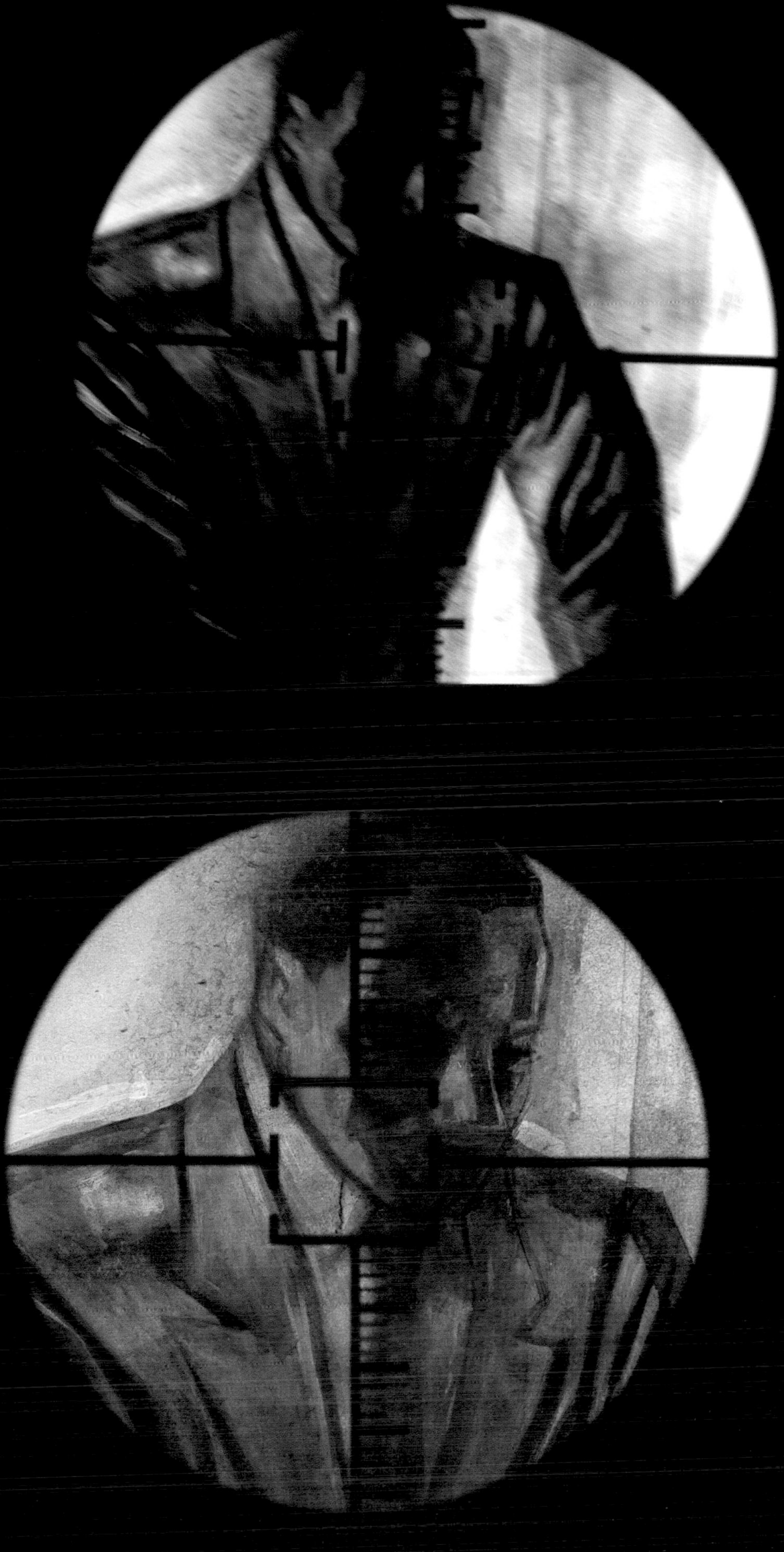

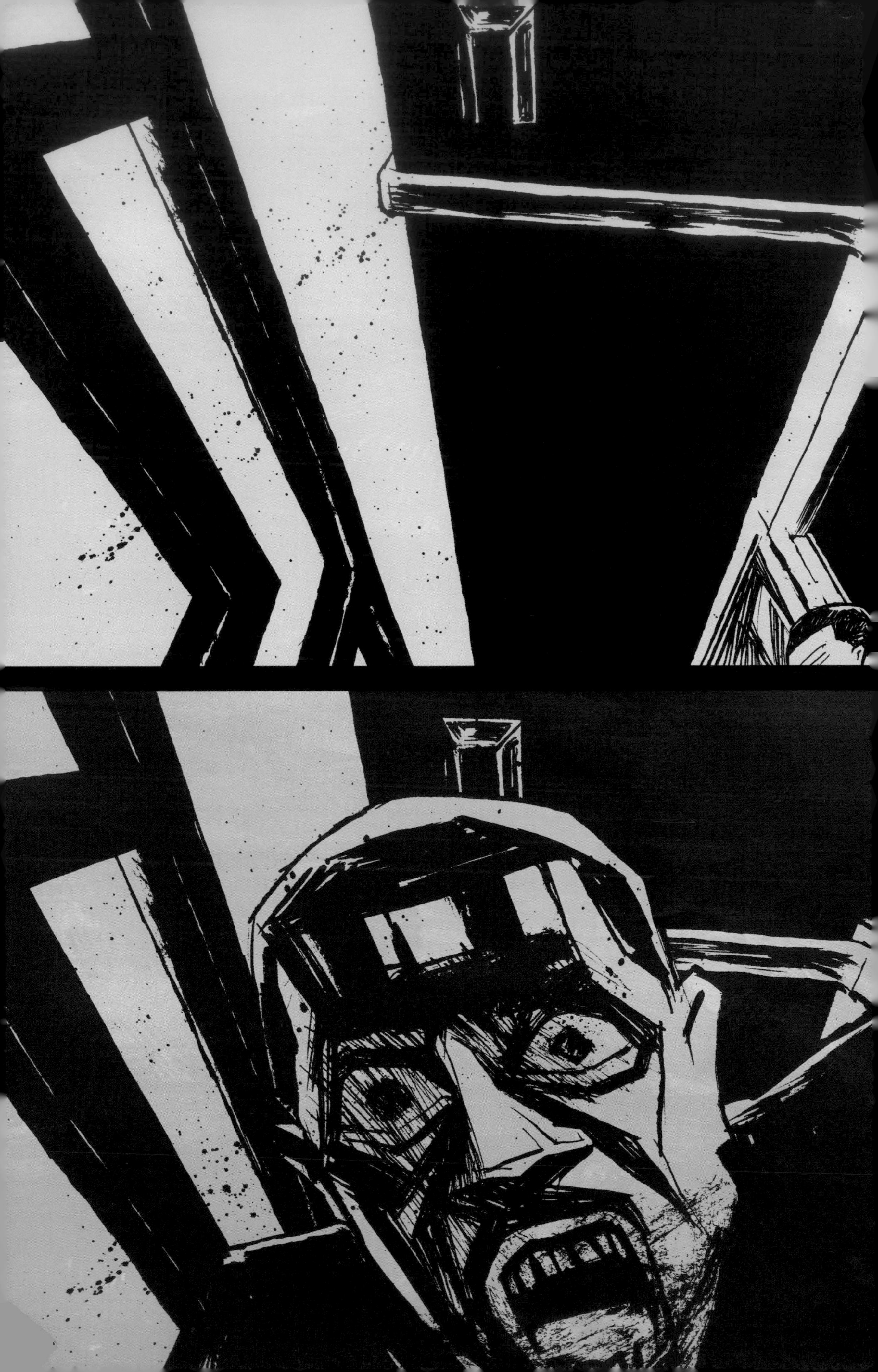

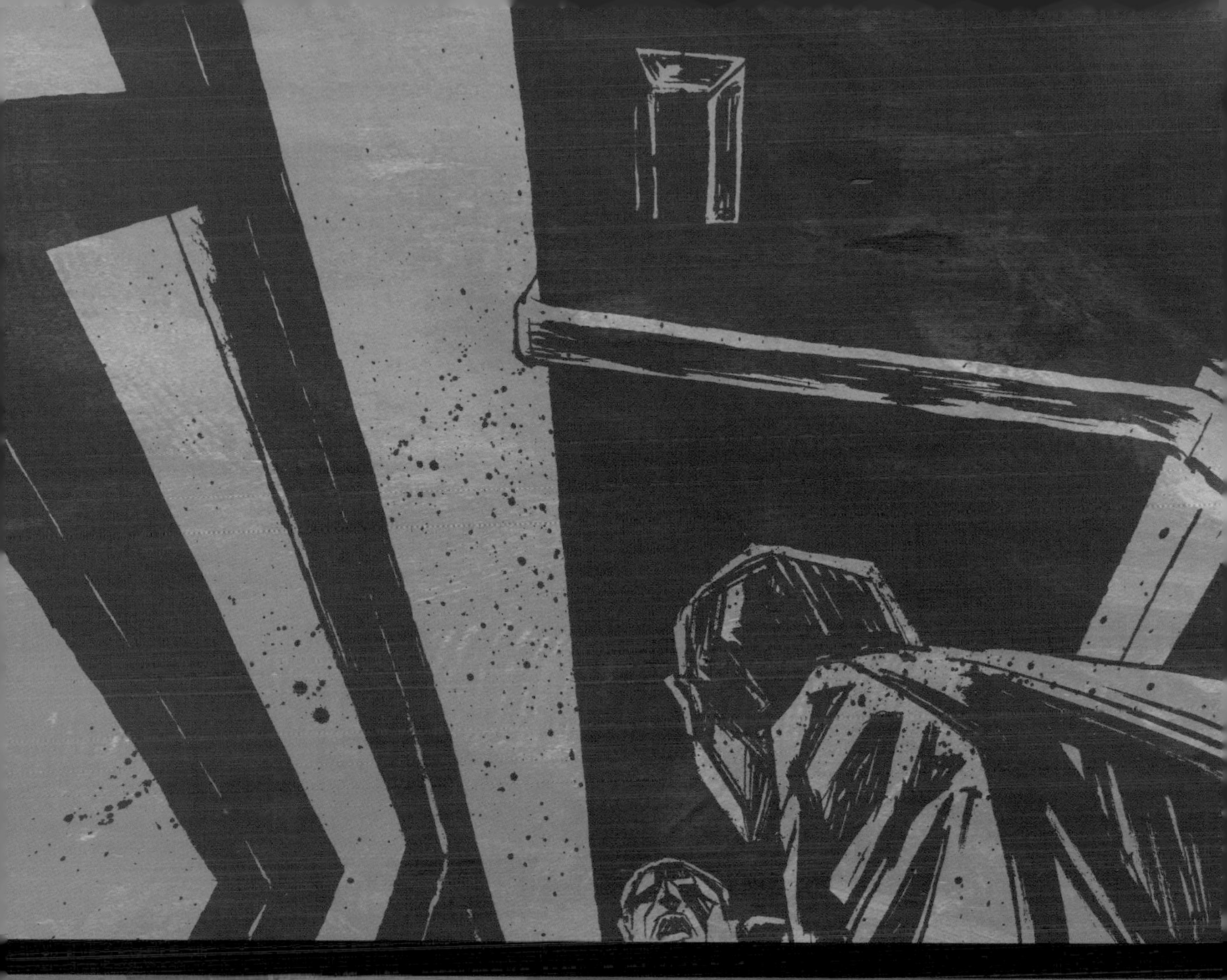

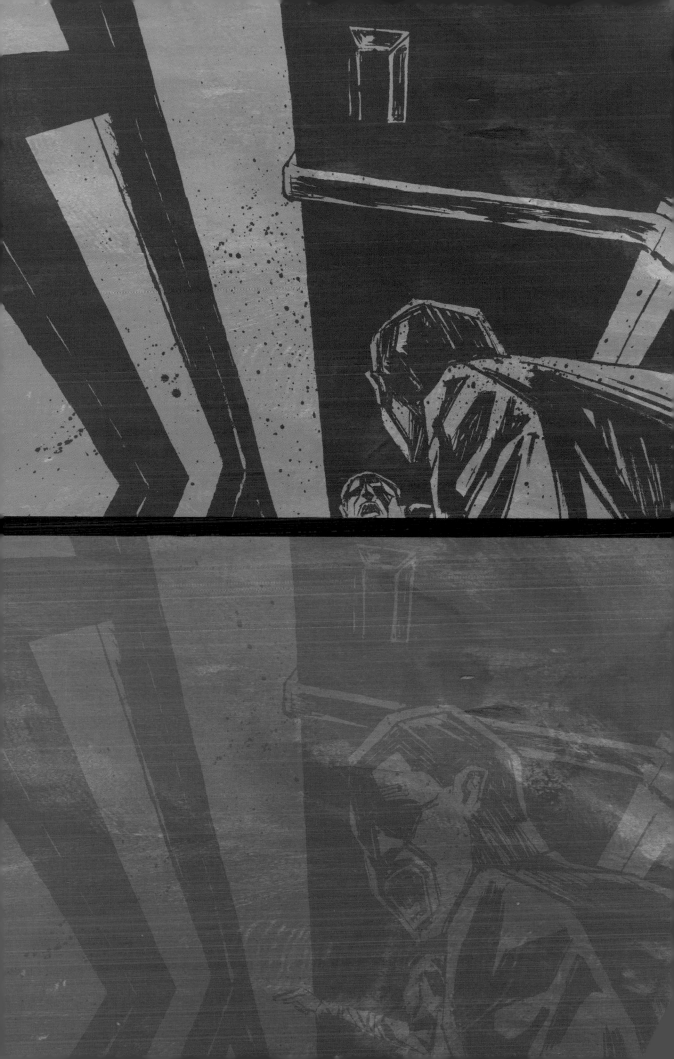

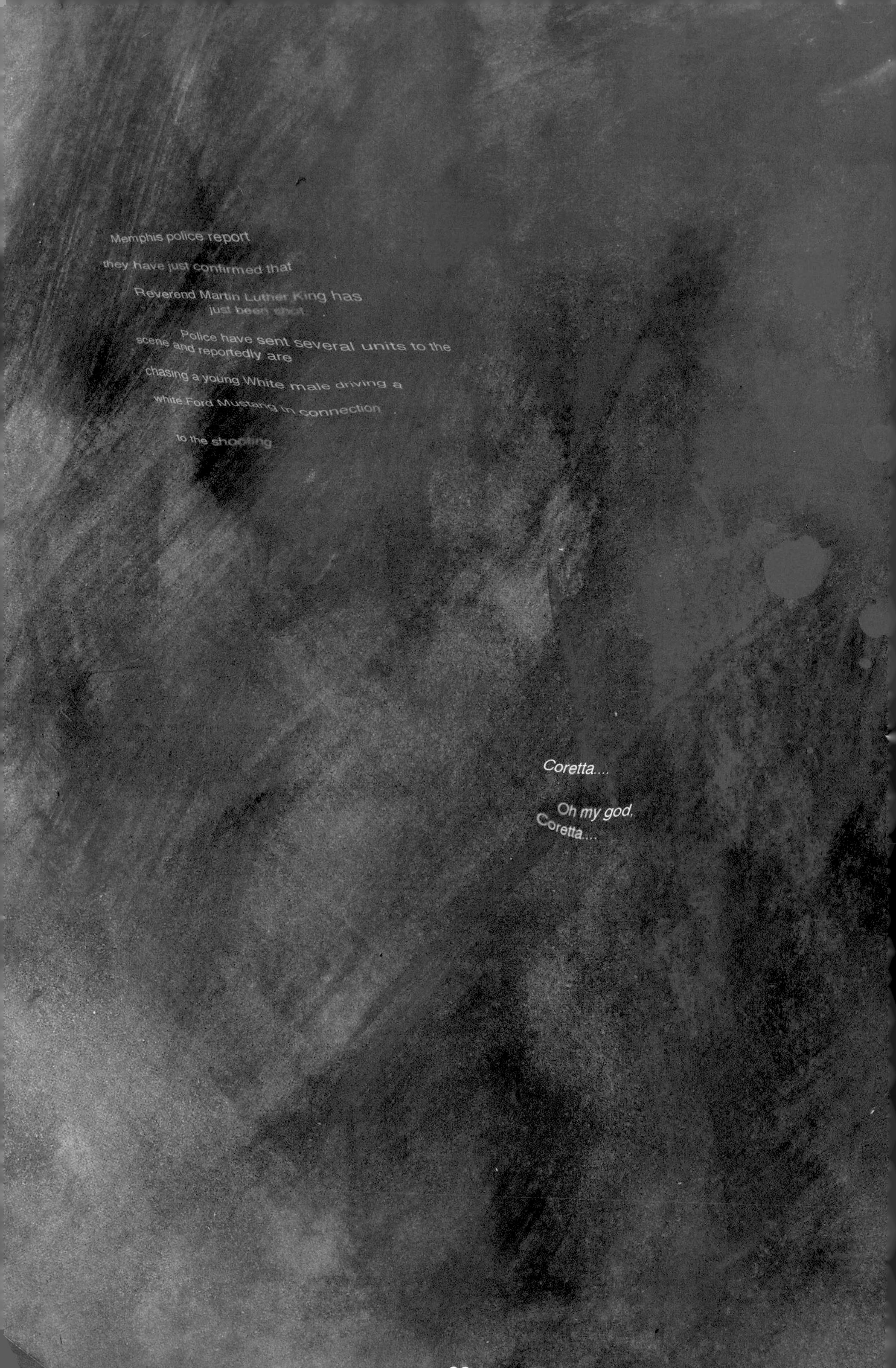
Memphis police report
they have just confirmed that
Reverend Martin Luther King has just been shot
Police have sent several units to the scene and reportedly are
chasing a young White male driving a
white Ford Mustang in connection
to the shooting
Coretta....
Oh my god, Coretta....

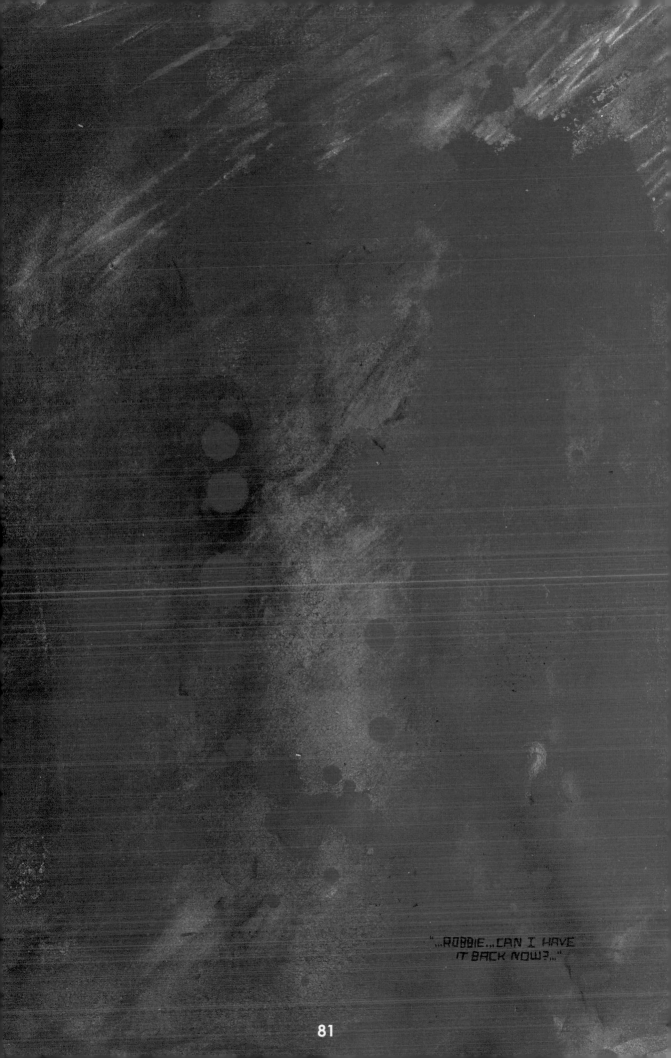

"...ROBBIE...CAN I HAVE IT BACK NOW?..."

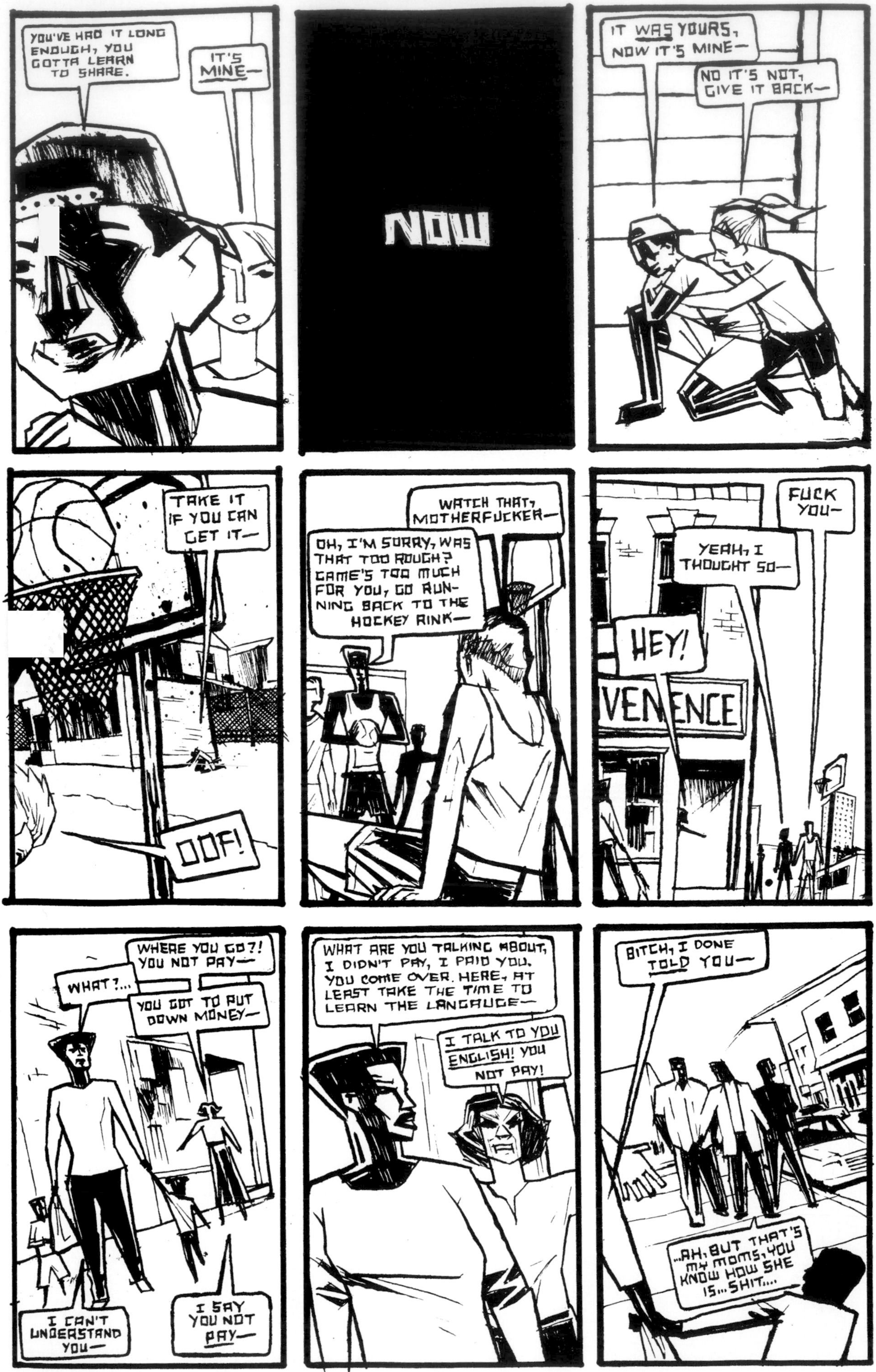

YOU'VE HAD IT LONG ENOUGH, YOU GOTTA LEARN TO SHARE.
IT'S MINE—
NOW
IT WAS YOURS, NOW IT'S MINE—
NO IT'S NOT, GIVE IT BACK—
TAKE IT IF YOU CAN GET IT—
OOF!
WATCH THAT, MOTHERFUCKER—
OH, I'M SORRY, WAS THAT TOO ROUGH? GAME'S TOO MUCH FOR YOU, GO RUNNING BACK TO THE HOCKEY RINK—
FUCK YOU—
YEAH, I THOUGHT SO—
HEY!
VENENCE
WHAT?...
WHERE YOU GO?! YOU NOT PAY—
YOU GOT TO PUT DOWN MONEY—
I CAN'T UNDERSTAND YOU—
I SAY YOU NOT PAY—
WHAT ARE YOU TALKING ABOUT, I DIDN'T PAY, I PAID YOU. YOU COME OVER HERE, AT LEAST TAKE THE TIME TO LEARN THE LANGAUGE—
I TALK TO YOU ENGLISH! YOU NOT PAY!
BITCH, I DONE TOLD YOU—
...AH, BUT THAT'S MY MOMS, YOU KNOW HOW SHE IS... SHIT....

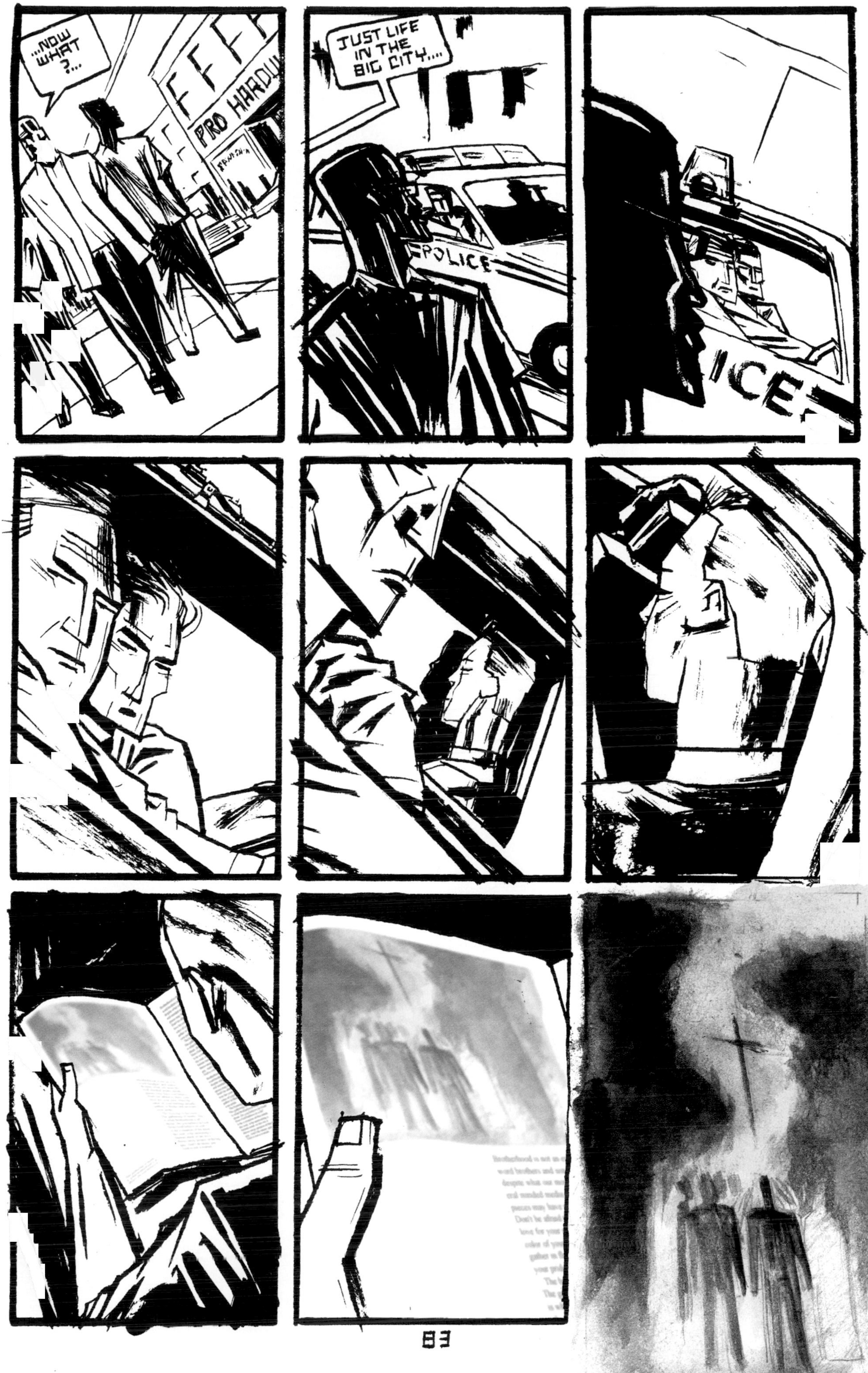
...NOW WHAT ?...
JUST LIFE IN THE BIG CITY....
POLICE

THANK GOD ALMIGHTY....

...WE ARE FREE AT LAST.

2003....

...Which makes it ten years since *King* volume one first hit the stands, eleven years since the night I first sat down with this project, scribbling in a notebook my ideas about what this book would become. I knew I wasn't ready for the job when I took it. I knew I didn't have the requisite experience, either as a cartoonist or as a living, breathing person. I hadn't lived enough, hadn't partied enough, hadn't learned enough, hadn't cried enough, hadn't felt enough pain.

My name is Ho Che Anderson. I didn't choose the name, and I certainly didn't make it up. I've come to terms with my name after a lifetime of having it made fun of, I've even embraced it as a means of developing a stronger character. But the truth is it's sort of an awkward moniker. It lurches out the mouth as opposed to rolling off the tongue. And given its historical antecedents, with it comes a certain vague pressure to live up to the sweep of greatness past, the greatness of history and its key players. I'll never be another Ho Chi Minh or another Che Guevara, and I'll definitely never be another Martin Luther King. But I can at least resign myself to my status as a bit player in life by rubbing shoulders with greatness through the pages of this comic book.

I'd call doing *King* an odyssey if the phrase weren't so shopworn. When I started I didn't expect this project to suck up over a decade of my life, but it did. It ran the gamut from feeling run of the mill to feeling important to feelng utterly irrelevant. Its alternately been a rush and a pothole on the road to happiness. There's a kind of sustained orgasm inherent in the act of writing and drawing comics, at least there is for me; not to wax too precious, but the chance to guide your own book has always seemed a rare privilege in my eyes— one I was thoroughly sick of halfway into volume one, ground down as I was by the weight of what I was doing and my inexperience at doing it. Maybe it sounds like I'm talking shit, but you try drawing two hundred pages and tell me how easy it is. By the time volume 2 rolled around drawing the book had become an out and out horror. As the years ticked by, producing merely a trickle of pages each season, the horror ripened and fermented. The burden of my eight hundred pound gorilla, knowing it lay in waiting, lurking impatiently behind me, at other times over the horizon just beyond my vision, silently observing the sparse triumphs and numerous missteps that constituted my existence. I couldn't see an end. It made me angry and it made me frustrated, and I hated doing it for a long, long time.

Somewhere along the way life transmogrophied into its latest incarnation. I looked *King* over and realized I'd been travelling with a faithful, if demanding, companion all these years; experiences had been assimilated and filtered through the comic without my having been aware. It had grown with me through the years I resented it and wished for its passing. What I'd come to regard as burden simply out of habit was now recast with powerful buzz potential, a fortunate by-product forged from the extra years of living, partying, learning, crying, and pain.

From the start *King 3* was the book I wanted to do the most. I'd be moving from the rural South to the brutality of Chicago's urban environs, a setting closest to the one I know intimately and love unconditionally; starting the comic in the summer of 2001 gave me a stiffy for a week.

Some will find this book too visually eclectic, too "all over the map," a charge I can't deny, and one I don't possess a reasonable excuse for except to say that after King 2 I felt I'd paid my dues, I'd earned the right to have fun, to do a book my way and no one else's. An exciting thought kept filtering through my mind, the notion that here lay a blank slate upon which I could do almost anything I wanted, my own personal playground. Because I approached the thing through virgin eyes and with brand new tools, all I saw before me was an ocean of possibilities and I dove right in. Perhaps the end result can be viewed as a tad self-indulgent but I can live with that because doing this book was a fucking blast: I haven't had this much fun doing comics since I was sixteen and burning with heat and passion for the form, and even then I don't think it was this good.

Maybe it's best you think of this book as fiction. Think of it as one man's riff on the life of another, part truth, part ephemera, a doorway into which I hope you will trip so that you might look around on your own. I gaurantee this is fascinating, rewarding stuff, if you care to see for yourself. Finally, for anyone interested, I apologize for the years I kept you waiting on the last two chapters, but only to a point because the way *King* ended was better then the way it began, if only for myself. I planned for a long time to show my ass to comics if I ever got this bitch finished—ironic that doing *this* comic has sparked an interest in sticking around for a little while after all. I'm stepping away from funny books for a spell, but if you're still out there in a year, maybe two, there are new books on the horizon.

See you on the other side.

Ho Anderson, 2002

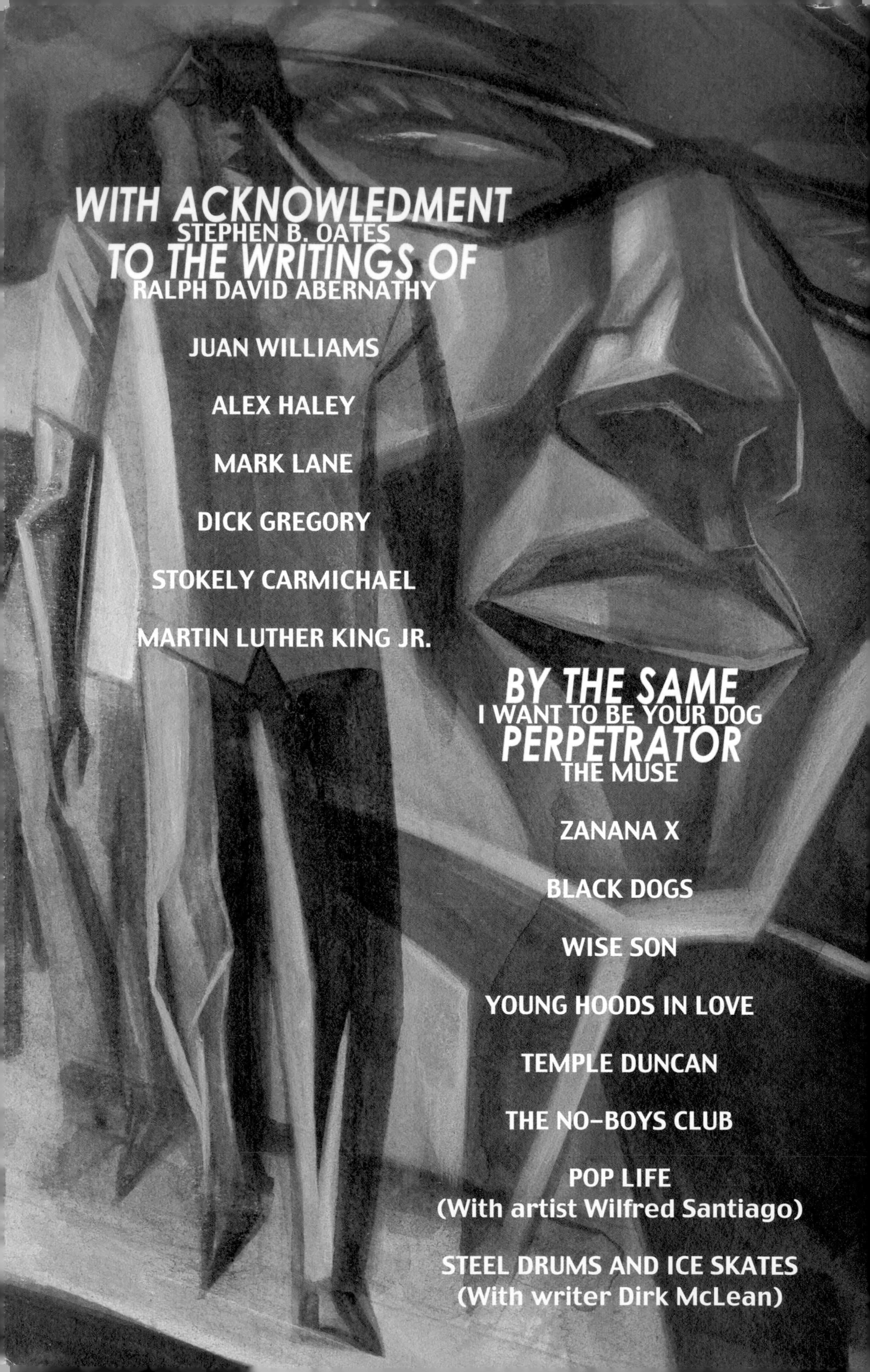

WITH ACKNOWLEDMENT TO THE WRITINGS OF

STEPHEN B. OATES

RALPH DAVID ABERNATHY

JUAN WILLIAMS

ALEX HALEY

MARK LANE

DICK GREGORY

STOKELY CARMICHAEL

MARTIN LUTHER KING JR.

BY THE SAME PERPETRATOR

I WANT TO BE YOUR DOG

THE MUSE

ZANANA X

BLACK DOGS

WISE SON

YOUNG HOODS IN LOVE

TEMPLE DUNCAN

THE NO-BOYS CLUB

POP LIFE
(With artist Wilfred Santiago)

STEEL DRUMS AND ICE SKATES
(With writer Dirk McLean)